Popular Cultural Studies

Series editors: Justin O'Connor, Steve Redhead and Derek Wynne.

The editors are, respectively, Senior Research Fellow and Co-Directors of the Manchester Institute for Popular Culture where this series is based. The Manchester Institute for Popular Culture, at Manchester Metropolitan University, England, was set up in order to promote theoretical and empirical research in the area of contemporary popular culture, both within the academy and in conjunction with local, national and international agencies. The Institute is a postgraduate research centre engaged in comparative research projects around aspects of consumption and regulation of popular culture in the city. The Institute also runs a number of postgraduate research programmes, with a particular emphasis on ethnographic work. The series intends to reflect all aspects of the Institute's activities including its relationship with interested academics throughout the world. Current theoretical debates within the field of popular culture will be explored within an empirical context. Much of the research is undertaken by young researchers actively involved in their chosen fields of study, allowing an awareness of the issues and an attentiveness to actual developments often lacking in standard academic writings on the subject. The series will also reflect the working methods of the Institute, emphasizing a collective research effort and regular presentation of work-in-progress to the Institute's research seminars. The series hopes, therefore, both to push forward debates around the regulation and consumption of popular culture, urban regeneration and postmodern social theory whilst introducing an ethnographic and contextual basis for such debates.

Titles already published

The Lads in Action

Social process in an urban youth subculture

David Moore

Addiction Studies Unit
School of Psychology
Curtin University of Technology
Western Australia

arena

Published by
Arena
Ashgate Publishing Limited
Gower House
Croft Road
Aldershot
Hants GU11 3HR
England

Ashgate Publishing Company
Old Post Road
Brookfield
Vermont 05036
USA

Typeset by Ms Jan Herrington
Edith Cowan University
Perth, Western Australia

British Library Cataloguing in Publication Data
Moore, David
Lads in Action: Social Process
in an Urban Youth Subculture
- (Popular Cultural Studies)
    I. Title II. Series
    306.0994

ISBN 1 85742 203 1 (Hardback)
ISBN 1 85742 204 X (Paperback)

Printed and Bound in Great Britain by
Athenaeum Press Ltd., Newcastle upon Tyne.

Contents

Contents

Acknowledgements

I have received much assistance and advice in the writing of this volume. I would like to thank the Department of Anthropology, University of Western Australia, for financial support during field research; Associate Professor Bill Saunders, Head of the Addiction Studies Unit, Curtin University of Technology, for financial support in the production of the manuscript; and Professor David Hawks, Director of the National Centre for Research into the Prevention of Drug Abuse, for allowing me time to work on the manuscript during my employment there.

I would also like to thank the following people for their assistance and advice: Noel Dyck, Suzanne Evins, Josephine Gooderham, Sharon Harford, Malissa Helms, Jan Herrington, Alison Marsh, Chris Mills, Philip Moore, Justin O'Connor, David Parkin, Steve Redhead, Hans Versluis, Charles Waddell and Derek Wynne.

Grateful acknowledgement is also extended to the following publishers for permission to quote from or reproduce copyright material:

Carfax Publishing Company for Moore, D. (1990), 'Drinking, the construction of ethnic identity and social process in a Western Australian youth subculture', *British Journal of Addiction*, 85(10), pp. 1265-1278;

Manchester University Press and Professor Anthony Cohen for Cohen, A. (1982), *Belonging: Identity and Social Organization in British Rural Communities*;

Omnibus Press of 8/9 Frith Street, London, W1V 5TZ for Knight, N. (1982), *Skinhead*; and

Smithsonian Institution Press for Kapferer, B. (1988), *Legends of People, Myths of State: Violence, Intolerance, and Political Culture in Sri Lanka and Australia*.

Three special debts of gratitude must be recorded: to my partner, Jodie Brown, and my parents, Mary and George Moore, for their unstinting support in ways too numerous to list; to Basil Sansom for helping me to make sense of skinhead social life, and for his Foreword; and, finally, to the young people who accepted me into their lives, some of whom I have disguised as Rhygin, Ace, Nutter, Rachel, Roy, Sue, Pete, Billy, Jack and Terry – to you I owe my greatest debt.

David Moore
Perth, Western Australia
September 1993

Foreword

In this book, David Moore argues that skinhead identity in Perth, Western Australia, is an assertion of British ethnicity on the part of youths who were born in England but who were transported by parents to an Australia in which their accents would always betray their British birthright. In the new country, the young migrants discover an Australian perjoration of their origins. For the youthful landed Pom, experience of Australian schooldays can be a running challenge. Will the evident Pom conform to Pommy type not merely as a speaker of accented English, but as a Pom who uses accented speech to whinge?

'Willie the Whingeing Pom' is the title of an Australian song, half pop half folk. The Willie featured in the song is a poor Will who has lost out from the start – he can hardly win when his very name is penis. As the lyric has it, Willie's is a besetting sin; he won't stop making Australian/British comparisons. And the Willie song celebrates a general phenomenon. In many contexts in Australia, the whingeing Pom rule is brought down to be applied as a rule of speech. It functions to prohibit any volunteered mention of the home country by a speaker of British origins. To begin a sentence with: 'In London ...' is already to have set off along the whingeing track. There is an underlying assumption. Metropolitan/Australian comparisons entered by migrants will generally be to Australian disadvantage. In the interests of survival in the face of unequal odds, wise migrants situationally relegate 'home' to the past; another time, another country.

David begins this book by describing the grand send off as a skinhead leaves Perth airport for London. Existentially, David has been in step though not ultimately in sympathy with the skinheads whose lives were made the subject of his study. He too came to Australia from England as a boy. In David's project, there has been a particular intersection of biography and community of study. This is worth pointing up for its bearing on the pursuits of both urban anthropology and the study of youth culture.

In her recent essay on the ways in which teenagers in an American city have appropriated punk and skinhead styles, Susan Willis ('Hardcore: Subculture American Style', *Critical Inquiry*, Winter 1993, 365-383) tells her readers that 'my daughter Cassie is my way into ethnographic research'. Appreciation of 'sub-culture American style' is mediated through the reports of a particular teenager, some of whose reporting must surely be conditioned by the fact that the chief interrogator is Mum. Biography enters Susan Willis's account. She notes that in a family that accommodates Cassie's punk-derived 'hardcore' look, a second sibling ascribes to a modified Barbie look, another is to be seen in black rap mode, while she herself establishes an older presence as a faded hippie. In all, there is a business of inter-generational inquiry. And there is vicarious investigation. 'The term Cassie and her friends use to define hardcore's ... dominant philosophy is *anarchist*. While patriots belligerently espouse American values, anarchists take every opportunity to piss on the government and anything that smacks of Americanism' (Willis, 1993:374, italics original).

The Lads in Action is a report based on both participant observation and collected representations. Throughout the book, the distinction between presentation and representation, enactment and reports about completed enactment, is kept to the fore. The difference between what people are seen to do and what they say they do is germane to the accounting. Had this not been so, David Moore would not have been able to write the analysis contained in one of his book's most notable chapters – the chapter called 'Memories', an account of the way in which skinheads create value by projecting shared history into the present to create a currency for exchanging the values that grant worth to protagonists in their circumscribed life-world. Vicarious investigation of sequestered happenings or impenetrable groups is better than no investigation at all. However, the anthropological use of the intermediary imposes distinct limits that derive from the distinction between knowledge *of* and knowledge *about*. Cassie renders her mother knowledge *about* hardcore style and anarchist ideology; Susan Willis is generally at a remove from the significant action, her knowledge *of* relevant scenes and happenings severely curtailed. There is a difference between reading culture as observed text and deriving culture from the texts of others.

Where moving with skinheads is concerned, that is, truly moving with the current skinhead generation, David Moore is finished up. He's past it. I note this finality further to point up the unrepeatable concatenation that allowed an anthropologically qualified but still sufficiently youthful David Moore to enter onto the skinhead scene and be there when the cops chased or the fights started. To the extent that David keeps up an interest in Perth skinheads, any further ethnography will largely be vicariously gleaned. I am pointing to a particular elusiveness of the stuff of life where youth are concerned. That elusiveness noted, I can celebrate *The Lads in Action* for its particular kind of opportunism. An investigator of the right age, is found in the right place, a place made right because that investigator's biography has existentially led to the formulation of a right sense of problem. In all this, *The Lads in Action* shares not a little with Elliot Liebow's *Tally's Corner*.

In her paper on American punks and skinheads, Susan Willis emphasizes styles of economic participation on the part of youth. Her subjects are young Americans who 'buy into' the styles they espouse and begin to present as hardcore, redneck, or whatever early on in their teenage years. She remarks 'the expansion of a teen labor market in the United States' (Willis, 1993:370). Participation in the teen labour market yields the disposable income that teenagers deploy as their very own earnings. Australia, in contrast, is a country of minimum wages, award wages and a labour ethos that has discouraged the proliferation of both part-time jobs and juvenile employment. Compared with the United States, Australia is a land of socially delayed maturity and economically prolonged teenage dependencies. The Australian/American contrast is worth noting as the relatively late entry of youth in Australia into gainful employment is a aspect of a scene in which becoming a skinhead belongs to the older teens and young twenties.

I return to the motivation of this study. Adopting the skinhead way is but one response to the terms of a continuing and nagging conversation that pervades Australia.

In this year of grace 1993, I have been trotting a five-year-old son around suburbia in Western Australia. We discovered a local butcher who purveys a line in Italian sausages. These became a favourite lunch-time food. We visited the butcher only to buy the favoured sausages. On the occasion of our fourth appearance, the butcher, knife in hand and looking every inch a butcher, weighed the sausages, wrapped them and then banged the package on the counter, distancing himself from that which he purveyed. He spoke to my eager child: 'So! you've really got a taste for Wog food?' And then the five-year-old was led into a protesting discussion about those things that can be counted as 'Aussie food for Aussie kids'.

Change of scene. It's the local shopping mall. We have an encounter with an elderly lady who greets us. I reply. Delfin is wide-eyed but silent. The lady then addresses the small boy directly. 'Young man, how are you'. Delfin replies in Aussie mode and he says: 'Good'. The interlocutor turns into Lady Bracknell, stepping straight out of the local dramatic society's recent production of *The Importance of Being Earnest*: 'Young man, I asked after your health, not after your moral condition'.

Delfin is experiencing public addresses that concern ethnicity. And these are given in the prescriptive mode. The butcher is a dinky-die Australian. He makes his own Aussie sausages for the traditional Aussie BBQ. The made-up Wog sausages are imported into his shop as a sideline. Our butcher is also the incarnation of a type of Aussie hero. He's the little man, a little battler, salt of earth and backbone of nation. His enemy is not only the supermarket but also those who give the *big* guys custom. He wants a committed and loyal clientele and isn't interested in occasional spot purchases. To attend on his shop and ask *only* for Italian sausages is either calculated insult or an act that bespeaks atheism (absence of sacred value).

Lady Bracknell is reasserting metropolitan English. 'Good' as a phatic response is actually not the normal reply to a 'How are you?' but the expected reply to the Aussie 'How're ya goin'?'. What I find amazing is the presumptuousness on either side. Butcher as cultural mentor or Lady Bracknell as reasoning exemplar, they both presume in their conduct of categorical relationships with anonymous strangers to act as missionaries.

The conversation concerning ethnicity, values and identity continues in this country to be conducted in vexed and unyielding terms. Children who hail from immigrant homes have to work to discriminate between codes and make self-conscious choices of expansion or restriction of competencies in a heteroglossic world. On the side of restriction and the narrowing of horizons, David Moore shows us unapprovingly but with great integrity of description how becoming a skinhead is one way to go.

Basil Sansom
Kalamunda
December, 1993

Preface

Nutter, a skinhead, is leaving Perth for England. He has planned the trip for several months, has tried to save as much money as possible, has avoided trouble with the police, and is looking forward to going 'home'. A large contingent of other skinheads, friends, parents and relatives has gathered at the airport to farewell him. In the corner of the airport bar a Union Jack draped from the top of a window eloquently expresses the ethnic identification of most of the well-wishers. At one table sits Jack, Roy, Ace, Scouse, Rhygin, Terry, two other skinheads and three young women; at another, Sandie, Rachel, Paul, Jane and assorted friends. A third table seats parents and relatives – the older generation. Others stand at the bar or between tables.

There is a carnival atmosphere – loud conversations, steady drinking, and the discovery of the latest news from those who have not been seen for a while. As the afternoon wears on some people become more emotional. I turn towards the bar to see Nutter and Jack standing together, arms around each other's shoulders, heads bowed in earnest conference.

The umpteenth nasal boarding call announces that it is time for Nutter to pass through Gate Four into the bureaucratic procedure prior to the boarding of the plane. People move slowly from the bar on the first floor of the airport building to the steps that will take them onto the concourse and Gate Four. As is now customary on these occasions, the party gathers on the balcony by the stairs to have its photograph taken. Over the railings hangs the Union Jack, the focal point of the group. The broken procession eventually reaches Gate Four for the final exchange of hugs, kisses and the shedding of tears.

As he moves to the gate and the uniformed customs officer, a teary Nutter turns to the assembly and, accompanied by a two-fingered V-sign (palm upwards), voices a shared sentiment: 'And this to Australia!' His gesture is met with a hearty cheer.

Introduction

This book is primarily an ethnographic account of the activities of the male members of the skinhead subculture, one of the more visible youth subcultures in Perth, Western Australia, as they are experienced and made sense of by these young men. I portray the skinhead subculture outside Britain and show how transplantation, and the experience of migration, affects the subculture. The style of my account differs radically from previous studies of English skinheads which, for the most part, fail to describe performance as a subcultural member.

In 1972, in a seminal article on English youth subcultures, Phil Cohen set forth a charter for the future study of youth, including skinheads. He proposed that a comprehensive analysis of any youth subculture involved three dimensions: the historical, the structural and the phenomenological. A number of sociologists, most notably those working at the Centre for Contemporary Cultural Studies, University of Birmingham (hereafter CCCS), accepted his challenge, but only in part. They produced sophisticated statements about the historical and structural (i.e., social class) dimensions of such youth groups as skinheads, mods, teddy boys and punks. They began their discussions with the working-class position of the members of these subcultures and then proceeded to analyse their meaning in macro-sociological terms.

These youth subcultures were viewed as forms of working-class 'resistance through ritual' to the dominant cultural hegemony and they signified the winning of cultural space within which young people, as members of these groups, could express themselves. However, with a few notable exceptions, these writers were noticeably silent about the subjective experience of everyday life as a member of one of these subcultures. In the 1980s, authors of youth culture studies, while criticizing and improving on CCCS work, remained reluctant to engage the issue of cultural construction and negotiation and thus did little to reverse this trend.

My aim is to provide a description and offer an analysis of what being a skinhead means to the skinheads themselves. What do skinheads do when they are being skinheads and what is the significance of these activities for them? It is their words and deeds that I have worked to capture. The end product is my reconstruction of their subjective reality. While the cultural and social dimensions of the Perth skinhead subculture may differ markedly from those of their English counterparts, my reporting of the underlying social processes which characterize this subculture and the analytical model I present in the final chapter are germane to an understanding of English skinheads.

Although wary of gross generalization, the description and analysis of social processes I present is also relevant to the activities of other youth subcultures, both in Australia and elsewhere. I have sought to present a microsociological account of how the members of an urban youth subculture order their social life and an interpretation of the reasons for the development and perpetuation of their distinctive style. While I have grounded my argument by reference to a specific empirical case, the underlying social processes I describe transcend particularities of time and place and are relevant to the analysis of youth in general.

By detailing the activities of Perth skinheads, I also wish to raise an issue germane to a consideration of ethnicity in urban Australia and in other multicultural nations. Since the early 1980s, the issue of ethnicity and of relations between different ethnic groups has sparked much public and academic debate about the 'true' nature and composition of Australian society.[1] A central assumption in these discussions is that the term 'multiculturalism' applies to non-English speaking people and/or non-British or Irish-born migrants and their descendants, and one of the central political and social issues is whether or not to limit new arrivals from southeast Asia. In the academic sphere, conferences focusing on 'Multicultural Issues' invite papers about Turkish, Croatian, Italian, Vietnamese and other migrants from non-English speaking backgrounds (NESB). The published strategies of the Multicultural and Ethnic Affairs Commission of Western Australia (1989, p. 15), a body established to provide advice to government, explicitly state this focus: 'Research is undertaken to facilitate policy development and analysis of issues affecting people of NESB in Western Australia'. Thus, when one speaks of 'ethnic' one is interpreted to mean 'non-Anglo-Celtic'.

In all this debate, those migrants from the United Kingdom and Ireland have not usually been thought of as 'ethnic' in the same way as, for example, people from southeast Asia. Because of the absence of obvious physical differences (e.g., skin colour or facial features) and the sharing of a common language, cultural differences are also assumed to be minimal or non-existent. Australia is described as being a predominantly Anglo-Celtic country as though these migrants are culturally identical to their Australian counterparts (and to one another). In fact, theirs is an 'invisible ethnicity' which only intrudes into the public consciousness during such events as the Ashes Test Cricket Series. This particular aspect of the multicultural debate is especially relevant to Perth with its high percentage of British and Irish migrants. The skinhead style represents a most visible adaptation to an issue passed over by those involved in this debate – being English in multicultural Australia. It serves as a refutation to those who argue that the sole cultural and social division within Australia lies between Australians of Anglo-Celtic origin and more recent arrivals from southern and eastern Europe and Asia. This treatment of 'English' as an ethnic category is rare in the social science literature.

The field experience

The idea to pursue research with skinheads arose out of my personal relationship with Rhygin (my closest skinhead friend).[2] I had known of him for about four years as an acquaintance of a sporting friend and had met him several times in this capacity. After this friend left Perth in 1983, Rhygin and I continued our association until we too had become close friends. He would visit me several times a week and inevitably discuss his latest skinhead activities. Through these informative visits he was able to enlighten me about many facets of the skinhead scenes in which he moved and provide me with considerable background on the personalities and events of recent months. When I began field research several months later I entered into situations and a network of relationships about which I already possessed some preliminary knowledge.

The data were collected during a nine-month period in 1984-5 and comprise information of three types: notes made after participant observation, stories collected during participant observation or in unstructured casual interviews, and arranged interviews. The usual method of recording information was through field notes which were made as soon as possible after arriving home from a day's or

3

evening's fieldwork. I never carried a pen and notebook relying instead on memory for recording events and conversations.

Most of my fieldwork time was spent with about ten skinheads who made up one group, most of whom resided in or near a southern suburb of Perth. The typical week of fieldwork consisted of outings on Friday and Saturday night, on several week days, and the occasional Sunday. Typical activities during fieldwork included playing pool and drinking in inner-city and suburban pubs and nightclubs, walking and sitting in Perth's central pedestrian shopping mall, walking between inner-city pubs, fighting, standing in groups talking, joking, and insulting one another, visiting people, drinking in homes, and eating in late-night fast-food places.

Rhygin and I had an arrangement that he would contact me whenever he was going out with his skinhead set. Therefore, the frequency of my involvement roughly matched Rhygin's. I came into contact with other skinheads regularly and frequently in the course of skinhead activity while moving with a set drawn from the ten. In this way, my movement within the skinhead subculture and English scene (see Chapter One) reflected the usual course of skinhead social life. However, I should point out that I moved mostly with what I have designated 'night skinheads' (see Chapter Three).

In order to gain access to a skinhead set, I initially negotiated for myself a role other than that of 'researcher' with which they could identify before revealing my research role (cf. Polsky 1971). For the first few weeks I accompanied Rhygin on his skinhead jaunts – drinking, spending afternoons in pubs playing pool, going to night-clubs, and finding myself in dangerous situations. (Another skinhead, Nutter, later joked that the skinheads should get me arrested before I finished 'hanging around'.) Being identified as a friend of Rhygin's clearly contributed to the relative ease of my entry. When the time came to inform them of the research, I had established myself as a part of the social landscape.

One incident proved particularly important in establishing rapport during the early stages of fieldwork. On the first Friday night of fieldwork I found myself, along with Ace, Paul and Rhygin, being chased down a central city street after an incident involving blame on both sides but odds of seven-to-four against us. The sprint came to an abrupt halt however when two policemen on patrol hailed us and asked us why we were making such haste. Ace and Rhygin, replied respectively, 'For our health' and 'Is there a law against running now?' We were threatened with a trip 'down to Central [Police Headquarters]' but were left with the warning that should there be any reports of misbehaviour, 'we'll know where to come looking'. The incident provided me with the most powerful of bonds – common experience. Moreover, common experience under threat, first from our pursuers and then from the traditional enemy, the police. For the rest of the evening, along with my three co-adventurers, I was included in the talk about the event. I had arrived on the skinhead scene.[3]

In the next chapter I describe the setting for my discussion, sketching in some of the basic dimensions of the Perth skinhead subculture and introducing the theoretical framework for the book. In Chapter Two I discuss the social organization of Perth skinheads to establish the dynamic context within which expressive social action is enacted. Chapter Three concerns style and in it I point to the inadequacies of previous writings on this aspect of youth. I then present the meaning of style for Perth skinheads. Chapter Four begins to detail some of the activities in which skinheads participate, notably fighting. In Chapter Five, I discuss interaction between skinheads and the members of other youth subcultures to address my own ethnographic data and to contend with authors who have presented subcultures as closed, static entities. Chapter Six continues this ethnographic examination by dealing with drinking patterns and Chapter Seven focuses on skinhead relations with young women. In Chapter Eight, which deals with the colourful stories told by skinheads to one another, I show how 'memories' shape categorical and personal identity. Chapter Nine, my conclusion, draws out the various strands in my ethnography to present a processural framework for the study of youth and the various implications of such a framework.

Notes

1. For examples of the various positions within this debate, see Blainey (1984), Burnley, Encel and McCall (1985), Castles, Cope, Kalantzis and Morrissey (1988), Markus and Ricklefs (1985), MacDonald, Hales and Associates (1989), and Shergold and Milne (1984).

2. The personal names used throughout the book (and those used to describe licensed premises) are pseudonyms. I have also altered minor details in the description of events (without damaging the overall integrity of the action described) to preserve anonymity.

3. Geertz (1972) similarly notes how, in the early days of his Balinese fieldwork, he and his wife forged a bond with their 'covillagers' during an incident involving police intervention in illegal cockfights.

1 The setting

English skinheads began their rise to notoriety sometime around 1967 in London's East End, their mode of presentation crystallizing into a recognizable style by 1968. The skinheads' immediate predecessors were the mods who split into two major streams: the art school mods, who were more concerned with fashion and clothing, and the 'hard mods' who became skinheads. Prior to and concurrent with the mod, had been a series of youth styles including teddy boy, Italianite, modernist, and rocker.[1] The original skinheads derived much of their style from a synthesis of two elements, the Jamaican rude boy[2] and their own white working-class base. The cropped hair, love of musical styles such as rocksteady, early reggae and bluebeat, together with the crombie coat, were all derived from rude boy style. The borrowed rude boy elements were fused with the 'caricature of the [white, working-class] model worker' (P. Cohen 1972), complete with industrial boots, Sta-Prest trousers, braces, and collared shirts, to produce a functional image. English skinheads favoured pubs as a focus for leisure activity and used alcohol as their main drug of recreation, along with occasional amphetamine use. Later, skinheads were to become publicly associated with violent assaults on gays, Pakistani immigrants and hippies, and with football hooliganism.[3]

Four themes were reportedly central to English skinheads: loyalty to other skinheads, specifically 'yer mates'; territoriality – whether it be the neighbourhood or football terrace; chauvinist, racist, loyalist, and anti-intellectual attitudes; and anti-authority – against the police and school, but usually not the family (Knight 1982). Further, two obsessions dominated – being authentic and being British (Hebdige 1982). Most skinheads saw themselves as 'straightforward blokes and birds, more honest than the soul boys, more working class than the punks and posers, rougher and tougher than the mods'

(Hebdige 1982, p. 28). Being British centred around the 'defensive assertion of whiteness just as Rasta is a celebration of the black cultural roots' (Hebdige 1982, p. 32). Faced with decreasing or non-existent job prospects and the perceived contribution of immigrants to this bleak situation, English skinheads retreated into patriotism – white ethnicity. Cashmore's *No Future* (1984) dealt with the resurgence of a more politically-oriented skinhead in the early 1980s amidst economic recession. In contrast to the 'mark one' skinhead, who targeted those thought to be threatening traditional ways of life, the 'mark two' equivalent embraced political theory of the Right to legitimize his actions.[4]

Studies of English skinheads, and other postwar English youth subcultures such as teds, mods and punks, belonged to a research tradition in which the starting point for analysis was the working-class structural position of the subculture's members.[5] Skinhead style articulated a concern with the aggressive reassertion of perceived traditional working-class values such as territory, community, and masculinity (Daniel and McGuire 1972). Politically, skinheads were involved in a struggle for control over their own life situation. Rather than accepting the dominant cultural meanings, they attempted to negotiate their own meanings which were symbolically expressed in subcultural styles.[6]

This body of work has been subjected to a number of criticisms.[7] McRobbie (McRobbie and Garber 1976) raised the issue of the absence of females from youth subculture studies and, more recently, has pursued a more data-based research programme (McRobbie 1991). In a related criticism, Frith (1984) noted that much of the CCCS work was based on media accounts (surprising, considering Stan Cohen's seminal work on press distortion of youthful activity) and that empirical research by Willis (1977) and McRobbie (1978) cast doubt on the much vaunted 'resistance' thesis.

Gary Clarke (1982), inter alia, objected to one of Hebdige's (1974a, 1979) central assumptions: the dichotomy between the 'true and authentic originals' of a subculture and the 'hangers-on'. Such a distinction came from viewing subcultures as pure, closed entities populated only by 'authentic' members and prevented any consideration of socialization into subcultures and of the processes involved in moving into and out of cultural scenes. An explanation of degrees of commitment was also absent. An explicitly structural definition of subcultural membership implied that all those in a specific class fraction were assumed to be members of the corresponding subculture. Conversely, all members of a subculture must automatically belong to the same specific class fraction. This assumption implied a false congruency between structural and cultural definitions of particular youth groups. The picture that developed from the CCCS studies was of static subcultures, the sizes and strengths of which did not vary, and whose members did not differ in their commitment and beliefs.

Clarke also noted that, historically, the CCCS perspective came into prominence at a particular intellectual and political moment, and reflected the personal concerns of scholars experiencing 'a mood of despondency arising out of the "1968 generation" and the relative weakness of recognizably political resistance in the early '70s'. The collapse of the Utopian dream and the failure of student radicalism 'led many Left academics to search for other groups pursuing a similar alternative lifestyle as themselves, particularly where elements of pre-figurative class consciousness may have been present' (G. Clarke 1982, p. 4). Waters (1981) further noted a related trend in the romanticization of working-class life by investigators who viewed members of subcultures as 'heroic figures' resisting the threatened breakdown of an idealized and idolized working-class culture.

More recently, Bell's (1990) study of Protestant youth culture in Northern Ireland, while explicitly working within the tradition laid down by Phil Cohen, questions whether an exclusive emphasis on social class is sufficient to understand youth cultures. Redhead (1990) argues that conventional subcultural analysis, which ties particular subcultures to specific socioeconomic and musical forms, fails to provide ways of understanding youth of the 1980s where there is a recycling and recombination of meanings, 'a supposed fluidity of positions, poses and desires', a theme also present in Gary Clarke's critique. Redhead argues for a greater emphasis on musical forms rather than a futile search for 'authentic' subcultures. Finally in the 1980s, under the onslaught of Thatcherism and the perceived need to re-evaluate much of the core intellectual apparatus of the Left, a 'new revisionism' (McGuigan 1992) has set in whereby authors such as Willis (1990) have moved away from an exclusively class-based argument to one emphasizing youthful symbolic creativity.

Despite the valid and numerous criticisms made of the CCCS, and of other related work produced by those not directly associated with the CCCS, Gary Clarke seems to have been one of the few writers whose criticisms open up the possibility of an anthropological perspective firmly grounded in ethnographic fieldwork. As early as 1982, anticipating Redhead's later analysis, he argued that since the advent of Punk, entire wardrobes of postwar styles had been 'exhumed, re-adapted and re-adopted' in a way which made conventional subcultural analysis almost impossible. Future studies would 'need to focus on what working class youths actually *do* and what the appropriation of clothing means to the youths themselves in these activities' (G. Clarke 1982, p. a). Despite his call, there is still little attention, at least in the United Kingdom, to the way in which particular youth cultures are created, negotiated and transformed, despite numerous statements about the need for ethnographies of lived experience.[8]

Turning to Perth skinheads, most are also drawn from the working class, if we define this category using structural criteria (e.g., socioeconomic status, level of education, occupation of parents), and so at least one profitable way of understanding their actions is as yet another working-class youth group, an Australian example of resistance through ritual. However, if one listens to the way in which skinheads describe, interpret and construct their social and cultural world, that is, to their 'definition of the situation', they do so primarily in terms of ethnicity. The absence of an explicitly working-class ethos makes the ethnic category ('English') a far more salient feature. By ethnicity, I mean the 'subjective process of group identification in which people use ethnic labels to define themselves and their interaction with others' (R. Cohen 1978). 'Ethnic' is 'the most general identity, presumptively determined by ... origin and background' (R. Cohen 1978 citing Barth 1969). To understand why ethnicity is such an important feature of the skinhead subculture we need to consider the social demography of Perth.

A multicultural city

In 1986, Perth, the capital city of Western Australia, had a population of almost one million people with a high percentage of these being migrants (Australian Bureau of Statistics 1986). These migrants arrived in waves, first from postwar Europe in the 1950s, 1960s and early 1970s, and, more recently, from southeast Asia (Houghton 1979, MacDonald, Hales and Associates 1989). At the 1986 Census, when the total population numbered 994,472, 32.1 per cent (318,876) of Perth's residents were born overseas of which 48.2 per cent (153,723 or 15.5 per cent of the total population) were born in the United Kingdom or Ireland. In the suburbs in which most skinheads live, British and Irish migrants comprise anywhere between 22.7 and 34.6 per cent of the total population (Australian Bureau of Statistics 1986). Commonly, in addition to the sizeable numbers of British and

Irish migrants, these suburbs contain a further fifteen to thirty per cent of residents also born overseas but not in the United Kingdom or Ireland.

Ethnic identification is a key social feature of multicultural Perth (MacDonald, Hales and Associates 1989). There are numerous business, cultural, political, religious, social and sporting groups, and other formal and voluntary associations with strong ethnic membership and affiliations. There are also Vietnamese Buddhist temples, Jewish synagogues, Moslem mosques, Catholic monasteries, a huge range of ethnic restaurants and people from almost one hundred different countries. Many football (soccer) clubs also give both formal and informal expression to ethnicity.[9] Their names express the ethnic origins of their founding supporters – Perth Italia, Floreat Athena, Olympic Kingsway, Stirling Macedonia, North Perth Croatia. More informally, these clubs are focal points for communities of like ethnicity spread throughout the Perth metropolitan area.

Large numbers of English, Italian, Greek, and Vietnamese migrants are concentrated within inner-city or suburban pockets as well as scattered more thinly over suburban Perth. In a government-funded study of Perth's inner city, the proportion of residents born overseas was almost forty-five per cent of the total population (MacDonald, Hales and Associates 1989). While scholars are divided over the nature of Australian egalitarianism, there is agreement on the lack of emphasis on forms of class-based deference in social interaction, except in status-related situations such as employer/-employee. Class differences are not represented as having the same import for everyday interaction as in Britain and other European countries (Oxley 1978). However, ethnic identity informs categorical relationships and comes to play a central role in personal identity (A. Cohen 1974, Mitchell 1956).

Perth skinheads

Perth skinheads represent an exported and modified version of the original skinhead subculture which gained national notoriety in England between 1968 and 1971. Perth's first skinheads began appearing around 1970 and their numbers swelled to a peak in the mid 1970s. Following the English Punk explosion of 1976, other youth styles originating in England (mods, teddy boys, punks) were transmitted by youth magazines and young English migrants to the streets of Perth. Many potential skinheads embraced these new (e.g., punk) or reasserted (e.g., mod) styles which led to the decline in skinhead numbers. Despite this influx of English styles, skinheads, with their distinctive cropped haircuts and Doc(tor) Marten boots, remain the youth subculture most widely associated with England.

The skinheads who are the focus of this book are aged between seventeen and twenty-one years (although there are skinheads as young as fourteen) and, with a few exceptions, are unemployed or only occasionally employed in unskilled or semi-skilled work. During the period of field research, Perth skinheads numbered about forty but this figure fluctuated. This number includes several marginal young men who perhaps thought of themselves as skinheads but who were not necessarily granted that status by other skinheads. Most skinheads still live at home with their parent(s). Consequently, group activity usually occurs outside the home, away from parental constraint. Some skinheads try living away from home but usually find their flat or house becomes an open-house to be used by other skinheads, invited or not. Being a skinhead is not a lifetime commitment and members of the subculture usually begin lessening their involvement with other skinheads in their early twenties, as other responsibilities (e.g., a long-term relationship or regular employment) assume greater importance.

Most Perth skinheads are English-born, having arrived in Perth in their early or pre-teenage years. Theirs is a youthful adaptation to the question of ethnic identity and there are other ways of expressing ethnicity which are more suitable to older British and Irish migrants such as membership of ethnic clubs (e.g., the Irish Club) or sporting organizations (particularly those focused on football). Skinheads not born in England usually play down this fact by developing vague English accents of indeterminate origins.

Skinhead is just one style comprising an extremely dynamic English-oriented youth scene in Perth, spawned by the high percentage of migrants from the United Kingdom and Ireland. Other styles include mod, teddy boy and punk. This wider English youth scene numbers in the hundreds. The educational backgrounds of the members of this wider scene vary from university students (medicine, science, arts) to labourers who have left school at fifteen years of age, although most are drawn from working-class backgrounds. Age also varies widely from fourteen years old to late twenties, even early thirties. Because of the interaction between members of the English scene, skinheads cannot be separated from the social milieu in which they move.

Membership of the English scene had become increasingly attractive to Perth youth since the dynamism of Punk in the late 1970s with the resulting profusion of music, dress and hair styles. Since then, there has been an Anglicization of some Perth youth styles, influenced by video clips of the latest English music groups, holiday visits to England to return with the latest clothing styles, and a number of shops importing this type of clothing direct from England. Thus, skinheads and the English scene of which they are a part are important in the overall Perth youth scene in stylistic and performative terms. They are responsible for, and a reflection of, much of the change of the past decade.[10] Skinhead, and English, clothing and haircuts have filtered to many non-skinhead and non-English youth. To take one clothing example – as recently as five or six years ago it was rare to see anyone but a skinhead wearing Doc Marten boots. Now, amongst those youth who frequent Perth's nightlife, they are common.

The way in which the potential skinhead comes to rediscover his ethnicity during adolescence entails a process of differentiation (Barth 1969, Wallman 1986). This process can be set in motion by being labelled a 'Pom' by Australian youth. In my discussions with several members of the English scene, similar patterns emerged. Although they had arrived in Perth at different times in their lives (one aged six years, three in their early or mid teens), all had been labelled 'Poms' on beginning school in Perth. Over time, these labels became internalized and, eventually, their uncertainties about their roles in a new country were converted into English patriotism. In contrast to the findings reported in this book, previous discussions of British and Irish migration to Australia either emphasize the ease with which children adapt to the Australian lifestyle (e.g., Appleyard 1964, Zamoyska 1987) or make no significant comment about this aspect. Only Richardson (1974) implicitly recognizes that the assimilation of British migrant children might be problematic.

The genesis and perpetuation of this rediscovery process, and its ultimate culmination in a group solution such as the skinhead sub-culture, usually requires reinforcement from other like-minded English youth who are easily available. Those who have chosen the skinhead option are often resident in geographical areas consisting of a high proportion of English migrants and/or are involved in sporting or other activities with sizeable numbers of English youth, for example, football clubs. For those English youths who do not become skinheads (or involved in other youth subcultures of English origin such as mods, teds, or punks) the reasons lie largely in the choice of an Australian peer group during the formative adolescent years.

Skinhead contacts with the Australian mainstream are limited. The skinhead moves with mostly English friends, returns home to English parents each night, might play football or watch others play football for an English-run club, and frequents the English youth scene for entertainment. He avidly follows the latest English football results and describes Perth only in pejorative terms. (There are always several people planning, or actually embarking on, a trip to England. The fact that they invariably return to Perth is usually overlooked or explained away with reference to the disapproved current racial composition of England.) In this sense, the skinhead is part of a larger subsection of the Australian scene, the English adult community. When the skinhead ultimately chooses to leave the skinhead scene, he retains his English ethnicity but expresses this ethnicity in less dramatic ways – such as retention of an English accent, perhaps greater involvement in a football club, and/or continued leisure activities within the English scene but as an ex-skinhead.

Bordieu (1984) has described the struggle for the ownership of cultural symbols as one way of establishing differentiation between social groups. The skinhead defines himself against the mainstream Australian world as a means of establishing identity. Skinheads perceive themselves to be very different from Anglo-Celtic Australians, as well as other migrants (e.g., 'wogs' or 'dings') or Aboriginal Australians ('boongs'). They nurture the old rivalry between England and Australia. This rivalry, in turn, is reciprocated by some Australians, in such expressions as 'whingeing Poms'. I once saw a T-shirt which featured the phrase 'Keep Australia Beautiful' on the front and 'Kill A Pom A Day' on the back. One could hardly hope for a more explicit and succinct statement of this rivalry.

Various diacritical features of this Australian mainstream, particularly the stereotyped 'ocker' character portrayed in such films as *The Adventures of Bazza MacKenzie* and *Crocodile Dundee I and II*, are selectively exploited by skinheads in order to distance themselves from Australian cultural models. Australian accents, clothing, and the game of Australian Rules Football are all derided. In particular, skinheads construct their stereotype of the Australian male by drawing on this cultural material and fashioning a derided and contemptible cultural construction – the 'moidy' (or 'Aussie' or 'bog').[11] According to skinheads, the young men who fall into this category commonly wear 'thongs' (Australian slang for the basic rubber sandal which has two strips which pass between the first and second toes and attach to the base on either side of the foot), have long, unkempt hair, speak with a broad Australian accent, wear flannelette shirts, drive large, powerful Australian-made cars (Ford or Holden) loaded with sports accessories (e.g., wide racing tyres, chrome wheel rims, aerodynamic body spoilers), listen to heavy metal music or Australian pub rock, and call women 'sheilas'. In the opinion of skinheads, the moidy represents an accurate depiction of most Australian males. Although skinheads share a structural commonality with those who comprise the moidy category, in their comparable working-class position, they explicitly distance themselves from them.

Beyond the sociology of appearances

With a few notable exceptions (e.g., Parker 1974, Patrick 1973), existing studies of skinheads and of youth subcultures in general suffer from one major flaw: they fail to describe performance. If we construct a distinction between youth studies which base their findings and argument on media reports, interviews, questionnaires, and such like, and studies firmly anchored in ethnographic research, the majority fall into the former category. These studies comprise a sociology of appearances, for they fail to make the crucial distinction between what people say they do (representation) and what they actually do (presentation). The findings and arguments of these studies contain little information about or discussion of the performative aspects of the respective study populations. Research method is an integral part of the equation and my emphasis on participant observation is one fundamental reason for the differences between my approach and that of many past studies. I take issue then with those authors who consider field research only good for producing 'Chandleresque qualities of prose' (Hebdige 1979, p. 76). It seems significant that the author of this phrase saw fit to omit any account of his own research methodology, presumably of the non-fieldwork variety.

I will differ radically from the literature on youth subcultures in my discussion of Perth skinheads. The study of skinheads is the study of a labile grouping (Sansom 1981) with lability manifest in the seeming absence of social form. A labile social grouping is one defined as 'liable or prone to lapse' (*The Shorter Oxford English Dictionary* 1988, p. 1165). Because there exists little form to guide skinhead social action in a regulative manner, the content of skinhead activity becomes the form. Skinhead activity is given shape by its constitutive acts and this is reflected in skinhead reluctance to categorize social action with explicit labels. Skinheads always tell a story of an actual event rather than describe institutionalized social forms and reputation is substantiated by expressive acts. By participating in skinhead activity for some time one learns about content. Form becomes apparent only through the accumulation of content. Such content is vested in stories which make the judgement of personal worth possible.

One question will dominate the book: how do skinheads organize their social and cultural world given its lability? To answer this question, I make recourse to the concept of 'style' and to Sansom's (1980, 1981) 'processural modelling'. For Sansom, the fundamental problem is to account for social continuity among Darwin Aboriginal fringe-dwellers when, according to the canons of traditional anthropology, they lack 'structural continuity, that is, some sort of continuity in the arrangement of persons in relation to one another'. Instead of such structural continuity vested in continuing arrangements, Sansom finds that Darwin Aborigines are people of labile social groupings whose associations with relevant others are characterized by their intermittent nature. They defy the notion of 'status' by entering into social positions that are 'self-liquidating' rather than fixed. These positions are highly person-specific, are not transferable to others, and lapse when the particular person dies or moves away. Consequently, social continuity is found in a conceptual order, in repeated ways of approaching oft-faced problems or 'business', and in 'rules for the provision, control and management of warranted social knowledge over time'. For Darwin fringe-dwellers, this conceptual order is retained in an Aboriginal verbal mode of discourse. By approaching social organization through language Sansom concludes that Aboriginal English provides the means for the perpetuation of a style for the arrangement of social relationships.

Like the Aboriginal fringe-dwellers of Darwin, Perth skinheads move in labile social groupings with constantly changing membership and relationships between these members. A skinhead may carve out a niche of his own through personality and physical prowess, but the position dissolves once its creator leaves the skinhead scene. Perth skinheads also have a conceptual order located in the perpetuation of cultural forms of and for behaviour. This conceptual order survives over time, despite ever-changing membership, by providing cultural guides to performance in varying social situations. These forms can be subsumed under the concept of 'style' and they supply ready-made guides to appropriate social action. These forms also undergo modification by successive age grades of skinheads with each skinhead interpreting and individually tailoring given subcultural beliefs to his own needs.

16

Unlike the Darwin fringe-dwellers, Perth skinheads use style rather than language to perpetuate these forms over time. When I refer to 'style' I mean the sorts of activities skinheads engage in, the way in which they set about organizing themselves for these activities, and the clothing they wear while engaging in them. By visual style I mean to specify the visual component of the overall style, for example, hairstyles, clothing, and tattoos. By performative style I mean the kinds of activities in which skinheads engage, for example, fighting, and the ways in which they organize to carry out these activities.

Whereas for Sansom's mobs language provides the means for the retention of order, the skinhead argot is sparse. For skinheads how one states something is less important than the statement's content. Asking three skinheads to describe the same event could result in three differently-worded answers despite the equal factual content. While there are words and phrases in common use to describe items of subcultural relevance, especially clothing and fighting, skinheads are not notable for articulating their social orientation.

Into the place of elaborate language steps visual style. I shall argue that visual style holds the forms for action. Different visual styles are associated with different modes of skinhead activity and corresponding groups. Instead of being described in elaborate speech, style of action is expressed in dress. The statement 'Me and Dave went to Darcy's' (an hotel frequented by skinheads) describes a scene with familiar modes of action and clothing, a category of style known to the skinhead in full possession of the knowledge outlining the range of possible activity. This knowledge is gained through participation in skinhead consociate activity. The coupling of style to scene also applies to members of other Perth youth subcultures. The process of linking scene to style incorporates many of the inner-city's pubs and clubs and Perth's other youth styles – rockabillies, teds, punks, and rockers, as well as 'straight' youth. Visual style means scene and states, to the initiated eye, complex clues as to the activity system and its members. For Perth skinheads, it is the non-verbal sign systems which are most important, supplemented by words. Hence, in this book, it is visual style which speaks.

Subculture

An interactionist approach to the concept of 'subculture' is provided by Fine and Kleinman (1979) who define four major problems with previous research. First, the authors of existing studies tend to confuse structural and cultural definitions of membership; thus, because the members of spectacular subcultures, such as skinheads, are often drawn from the working class it is assumed that their cultural beliefs automatically reflect wider working-class values. Second, there is a lack of meaningful referents with few studies defining what it is they mean by 'subculture'. The third problem is that many past studies of subculture are synchronic and do not allow for constant flux over time. Existing accounts reify culture and assume the subculture to be an homogeneous and closed social entity isolated from larger society. Finally, sociologists have tended to portray subcultures as having a central core of values organized into a system. These central values are somehow external to the sub-culture's members who are constrained by them. Specific cultural elements such as particular behaviours, norms and artifacts which are most important for interaction are neglected in analysis.

Fine and Kleinman present a reconceptualized view of subculture which focuses on the interacting group. This group is made up of smaller groups interacting with one another through a large number of interlocking social connections. A common world of discourse is constructed by the spread of cultural information and behaviour options through this social network which serves as the referent of the subculture. Cultural content is modified and transformed through negotiation between the small groups in the network. Therefore, 'subculture' serves as a construct covering the community occurring within interlocking groups and the knowledge and behaviours shared by these groups. The extent of the subculture is found at the boundaries of knowledge within the social network.

The transmission of cultural knowledge between interlocking groups occurs in several ways. A person may hold multiple member-ship of several groups simultaneously and transmit information between them. 'Weak ties' (Granovetter 1973), which describe the links in a network which is never bounded, provide access to inform-ation and resources available through persons outside usual contacts. Information may also be spread by persons who perform structural roles for several unrelated groups, for example, the drug dealer for several different drug-using groups. The mass media also afford contact with several groups at once, either through specific media aimed at specialist audiences or through mass public communications. Some members will identify and therefore be more committed to a particular subculture than other members. Identification varies along two axes: centrality, or degree of commitment, and salience, or frequency of identification. Those persons whose commitment vacillates move in and out of, and between, subcultures facilitating dissemination of information in a dialectical process. Finally, the societal response provides another avenue for the transmission of knowledge.

Fine and Kleinman advocate an ethnographic and qualitative approach which involves an emphasis on those behaviours, symbols, and artifacts regarded as important by members of the interlocking groups. Conceptualizing subculture as a process which involves the creation, negotiation, and spread of subcultural items offers a framework within which research can be conducted. An interact–ionist and phenomenological conceptualization of subculture addresses many of the theoretical and methodological limitations in current approaches to youth and informs the way in which the term 'subculture' will be used in this book.

'Time-out' and belonging

Becoming a Perth skinhead is a 'time-out' response to mainstream society and culture. I say 'time-out' because being a skinhead does not represent a permanent adaptation but rather a phase of life, usually beginning in the early teens and ending in the early twenties. Youth is a liminoid period between early adolescence and adulthood responsibility where meaning is made and identity claimed. Skinheads themselves see membership of the skinhead subculture as a passing phase, symbolically ended by the growing of cropped hair – 'It's about time you grew your hair, you're getting too old for all this'. Being a skinhead is seen as a time of adventure and excitement, trysts with the opposite sex, of fighting and helping your mates, of nightclubs and pubs, and of 'good times' to recount later when you reflect on what a 'lad' you were. It provides a chance to postpone for a few years the inevitable submission to the inherent responsibilities in being 'grown up'.

This time-out response can be split into two analytical categories or degrees of commitment: 'day' and 'night' skinheads. 'Day' corres–ponds to the core skinhead, usually unemployed, whose embracing of the style is total. His commitment is unquestioned and the tattoos prove it. How do we integrate this group with the 'night' skinhead, one who might have a job and who socializes only on weekends, but whose status remains untarnished by this seeming obeisance to the mainstream? I will borrow Anthony Cohen's (1982) concept of 'be–longing', that is, the perception of membership of a particular group, expressed in specific shared understandings about cultural and social differences and reflected in behaviour. For Cohen, writing about rural Britain, five elements comprise belonging: commonality, a narrow range of relationships, idiom, trends of social organization, and locality.

For skinheads the generative point of belonging derives from their commonality – in their English ethnicity and as youth in industrial society – and in their trends of social organization, that is, the way in which they work together. For the skinheads, this 'way' can be categorized as 'expressive' in that it fulfils certain personal require–ments – to make life meaningful and to facilitate the construction of identity. Being a skinhead is expressive in that power lies in the control of the self. The products of this expressive milieu, such as reputation, status, and having many 'good nights' to remember, are not transferable but only have worth in Hannerz's (1980) recreation domain. Only the stylistic declaration of being a skinhead, and thus stating one's prime identity, gains public recognition.

I have already presented the labile framework in which expressive social action occurs and noted my dissatisfaction with existing des–criptions of youth subcultures. What is needed is a sociology of presentation, social action and performance. In this book, I will examine the notion of skinhead authenticity and its link with 'memories': what is it that skinheads strive to be collectively judged as? My task is made difficult by the absence of structure and by the skinheads' refusal to invent categories. Instead, skinhead authenticity is rooted in participation and the proof of participation lies in stories about performance. What follows is a book about what it means to be a skinhead where meaning is dialectically established through the interplay between performance of consociate activity and judgements brought down on such performance.

Notes

1. For discussions of teddy boys, see Fyvel (1961) and Jefferson (1973); for mods, see Barnes (1979) and Hebdige (1974a); and for general discussions of the evolution of postwar British youth styles, see Brake (1980), Cashmore (1984), Hebdige (1979), and Redhead (1990). Richard Allen has written a number of fictional works on skinheads and other youth styles in England, for example, Allen (1970, 1971, 1972). For an account written by a skinhead and featuring enormous detail on music, clothes, activities, youth politics, riots, and so on, see Marshall (1991).

2. The rude boys were originally rural Jamaican youth who had settled in the shantytowns of Kingston. During the 1950s, with the migration of West Indians to London, these rude boys made

their first appearances on council housing estates. Much of the mod and, later, the skinhead clothing styles were borrowed from these original rude boys (see Hebdige [1974b] for a fuller account). In the late 1970s, a new breed of rude boy flourished, riding on the wave of new music bands such as The Specials. They were white and seemed unaware of the West Indian origins of the rude boy style (see Cashmore [1984] for details about white rude boys).

3. For a brief but interesting discussion of football violence which differs from the view offered by J. Clarke (1973b) and Taylor (1971), see Middleton (1986).

4. See Hewitt (1986) for confirmatory evidence. For a skinhead account of youth politics, see Marshall (1991).

5. For example, Brake (1974), J. Clarke (1973a, 1973b, 1974), Hebdige (1974a, 1974b, 1979, 1982), Jefferson (1973), Willis (1977, 1978), the general papers of Roberts (1973) and Clarke and Jefferson (1973a, 1973b), and the collections edited by Hall and Jefferson (1976) and Mungham and Pearson (1976).

6. A tradition of ethnographic studies of youth in Australia is poorly developed (e.g., Pearson 1979). The best of such studies, Walker's (1988) *Louts and Legends* is not grounded in a description of the social organization of youth groups. White (1990) and Stratton (1992) provide theoretically elegant studies which take on board much of the overall conceptual legacy of the work of the CCCS while overcoming at least some of the criticisms of such a perspective. Although White documents some of the responses, both collective and personal, of different categories of youth to structural conditions (e.g., Willis 1977, Wrennall 1986), these structural conditions are themselves presented in a reified manner. Just as Willis (1977) describes the ethnographic complexity of the school culture of working-class boys but chooses to caricature 'the [capitalist] system' in which they live, the arguments of White and Stratton depend on an uncritical acceptance of structural conditions which are left ethnographically unexamined. As Marcus (1986, p. 186) points out, the system that oppresses one group is another's cultural form.

7. Other critiques can be found in S. Cohen (1980), Foley (1988), Laing (1985), Marsland (1978), McRobbie (1980), Sato (1991), and Walker (1985, 1986).

8. One recent exception to this trend, from outside the United Kingdom, is provided by Sato (1991) in his ethnographic analysis of an urban youth subculture in Japan.

9. In Australia, 'football' is commonly and officially known as 'soccer' to distinguish it from other football codes. Perth skinheads, as well as English migrants in general, tend to use the term 'football' rather than 'soccer' to describe association football; a linguistic example of the declaration of English identity and origin.

10. The latest in this long line of British imports is the rave phenomenon, although coming too late to be included in this work.

11. Perth skinheads derive the term 'moidy' from exaggerating the Australian pronunciation of 'mate'.

2 Scenes, venues and eras

How labile youth subcultures form into groups, and the nature of these groupings, has been a much neglected area of research. American studies tend to focus on the structural positions in the highly-organized 'gang', with formal positions such as President, War Counsellor and Weapons Counsellor (e.g., Keiser 1969, Yablonsky 1963).[1] Australian studies of youth offer little analysis of social organization (e.g., Pearson 1979).[2] More recently, the English subcultural theorists fail to describe any organizational characteristics, a flaw which reflects their ethnographically weak position. There is a need for an analysis which can take into account not only structural characteristics but also the dynamics of group formation over time.

Despite several sociological and anthropological studies to the contrary, the description of adolescent groupings as 'gangs' continues in both the mass media and popular characterizations, as well as in some academic circles. Probably the first academic attempt to lay the gang myth to rest was Yablonsky's development of the notion of 'near-group' (1959) and his discussion of the characteristics it lacked for true 'gang-ness'. The near-group was characterized by 'diffuse role definitions, limited cohesion, impermanence, minimum consensus of norms, shifting membership, disturbed leadership, and limited definition of membership expectations' (Yablonsky 1959, p. 109). However, he chose to ignore social processes and labelled the leaders of his near-groups 'psychopathic'.

In 1966, Downes wrote an article entitled 'The Gang Myth' which neatly stated his objections to the notion of 'gang' when applied to English youth. He argued that the situation in the United States was still confusing and that there was a great diversity of group frameworks for serious delinquency, ranging from structured gangs to near-groups. In England there appeared to be a much narrower range of variation; gangs were virtually non-existent, but mobiliz-ation into near-groups was possible in extreme situations. Downes stated his support for Yablonsky's near-group and cited the studies of Scott (1956) and Farrant (cited in Downes 1966) to lend weight to his position that English youth was gangless. Patrick (1973), another student of youthful behaviour (in Glasgow), concurred with Downes arguing from his own extensive literature survey of American and British material. He concluded that there were significant differences in the organizational features of the more casual English youth groups as opposed to the more structured American and Scottish (Glaswegian) groups. More recently, theorizing about the social organization of youth collectivities has centred around the concept of the 'peer group'. In the United States, some refinement has been attempted with the differentiation of 'peer' and 'friend' within these groups, and the introduction of 'peer clusters' (Oetting and Beauvais 1988). Like the notions of 'gang' and 'near-group', the concept of 'peer group' remains essentially static in its framework and app-lication.

We encounter problems however when examining many of the studies made of so-called gangs, near-groups or peer groups. As is so often the case, discussion of the performative aspects of the group members is largely absent from the accounts. While there appear to be organizational differences between American and Scottish gangs on the one hand, and English groups on the other, we are given no clue as to the consequences of this difference for day-to-day interaction. For Perth skinheads, the concept of 'gang', as a struct-ured hierarchical group with definite membership, leadership and territory, has little relevance. Organized gang structure and lability are antithetical.

As Sansom (1981) has outlined for Darwin fringe-dwellers, Perth skinheads form labile social groupings characterized by fleeting associations and self-liquidating social positions and identity. This means that they form and re-form their relationships frequently. The pattern of association is characterized by clusters of close relationships amidst a sea of weaker ties, some of which are 'bridging' (Granovetter 1973, 1983) and thus provide links between the clusters. A skinhead may have one or two close friends, or regular consociates, a small circle of others seen most frequently who are also fairly good friends, or intermittent consociates, and then know a vast multitude of others within the subculture who are merely nodding acquaintances, or occasional consociates. However, these groupings can, and do, change rapidly. Friends are drawn from within a limited social universe and can immediately become 'mates'.[3] In this respect, the skinheads resemble the African American streetcorner men of Washington depicted in the book *Tally's Corner* (Liebow 1967) where two men who have only just met can become 'up tight' (close friends) within a short period.

If Perth skinheads do not move in gangs, what form do their groups take? To answer this question, I want briefly to sketch the constant changes in relationship between persons and groups through examining the career of one skinhead, Rhygin, and then move on to discuss this dynamism using the notions of action-set and quasi-group (Mayer 1966) and of scene, venue and era.

Rhygin's career

We join Rhygin in 1980, aged sixteen and in his final year of secondary school. Rhygin and two of his closest friends, the extroverted Bob and the more phlegmatic Adrian, form an obviously English trio. The high school has a large proportion of Australian students and this ethnic difference provides the basis for much of their interaction with other students. Between finishing school and beginning university (Australian summer, 1980-81) the maturing trio see *Quadrophenia*, a film set in 1960s England and focusing on the mods and their world – one of sex, drug use, and violence. To the three young men, the film is exciting. Bob and Rhygin enrol in one of Perth's universities and begin their studies in 1981. Adrian elects to defer his studies for a year and works, saving money for a holiday in Europe and for his studies the following year.

After hearing about the activities at a particular inner-city tavern (at this time one of the focal centres for the English scene), particularly with respect to relationships with the opposite sex, the threesome decide to see for themselves. Early in 1981, Rhygin and his two friends meet some members of the English scene by frequenting this tavern, accompanied by several young women met through attendance at university. Rhygin also meets a recognized social trendsetter, Jeff, and, through Jeff, meets members of another set. Rhygin's social network continues to expand and by the end of 1981 he is recognized as a regular at the tavern, has secured a reputation for being unpredictably entertaining and knows many of the mods, skinheads and ex-skinheads who also frequent the tavern.

After their first year at university, Bob and Rhygin decide to leave and find employment. During 1982 Adrian commences university studies, ceases his tavern visits, but continues to see Rhygin and Bob in other social settings. Rhygin's knowledge of personalities within the English scene is expanding. Bob, after being a skinhead, becomes more 'moddy' as time passes, much to Rhygin's disgust. Rhygin dislikes the flamboyance of the mod style, despite being friendly with several mods, and he continues to pursue his skinhead line. Bob and Rhygin begin to drift apart with Bob opting more and more for a regular 'girlfriend' and the mod style, perhaps because of the emphasis on clothing and music rather than fighting. Shortly afterwards, Bob marries and steadily decreases his involvement in the scene.

In 1983, Rhygin renews his acquaintance with a prominent skinhead, Len. Through Len he meets Mick and Joe, recently arrived from Melbourne with a fund of skinhead stories from that city. Rhygin begins seeing Mick and Joe and their 'lot' (he already knows some of them) with increasing frequency. He is with this group when they meet Ace, Nutter, Smithy and several other skinheads at the Ipswich Hotel. A fight occurs between Smithy, one of Ace's set, and an Australian opponent, and Rhygin's group lends physical support to the ensuing melee. This aid forges a bond between the two factions and becomes enshrined in the stories repeatedly told about the event.

In 1984, Rhygin, thoroughly disillusioned with life in Perth, follows a pattern common amongst skinheads and leaves for England, unsure of when he will return.

On his return from England later in 1984, Rhygin strikes up a friendship with Harry, a skinhead particularly prone to finding himself in violent altercations. Through Harry, he also meets Chris. Chris is a rockabilly and chooses alternative nightlife to either Rhygin or Harry. Harry has already booked a one-way trip to England some time before. The timing of Harry's trip turns out to be perfect as the police are looking for him 'to help with their inquiries' into an assault. After Harry leaves for England, Rhygin associates more with Chris who is slowly swapping his rockabilly style for that of a rude boy.[4]

About two months later, Ace's girlfriend, Sharon, whom Rhygin knows from his local pub and associated scene (she lives near Rhygin), phones him. She is worried because the impressionable Ace is increasingly associating with Nutter, Roy, and Pete, a trio well known for their propensity to get 'into trouble'. Rhygin responds by visiting Ace. Ace's stated reason for seeing Nutter, Roy, and Pete is that Scouse and Little John, his two closest friends, both have girlfriends and Smithy is 'out of it' (no longer a skinhead). No other friends lived in the immediate geographical area. In effect, he is compelled to associate with the troublesome trio to maintain his skinhead links.

Rather than succeeding in advising Ace to stay out of trouble, Rhygin also begins associating with Nutter, Pete and Roy. Meanwhile, Rhygin and Chris have girlfriends who are close friends and this contributes to Rhygin's increased association with Chris. Rhygin usually socializes with Chris during the week (as he lives much closer to Rhygin than Ace) and Ace, Nutter and the others on the weekend nights, usually meeting them in the city. However, Chris, in his desire to emulate Rhygin, begins to irritate Rhygin who consequently switches his focus to Ace and his set.

Meanwhile Rhygin has also continued his patronage of the local pub and meets a new circle of people, all members of the English scene in varying degrees. He increases his association with this local group, eventually introducing its members to Ace's set. However, the two sets never see a great deal of one another, the association being a somewhat uncomfortable one. Rhygin continues to see Ace but not as frequently as he had done in the months before, preferring to spend more time with the local group.

By 1985 Rhygin is beginning to grow his hair and his boots gather dust. He has been a skinhead for approximately five years. While still frequenting the inner-city pubs and nightclubs, he now wears the style of the 'ex-skin'. He is no longer a skinhead but takes his rightful place as a known identity, a reputation that is reward for the investment of his youth.

The formation of groups

One way of modelling the social process evident in Rhygin's story is through the constant interplay between three levels of social organization: the category, the action-set and the quasi-group (Mayer 1966). A skinhead relates to all other skinheads at the categorical level, that is, they share certain interests and behaviours in common. All skinheads, by the act of declaring themselves skinheads and being accorded that status by other skinheads, belong to this same broad category. From within this category, a skinhead recruits perhaps four or five other skinheads to be part of an action-set which engages in a specific event, such as a drinking session. By superimposing a series of successive action-sets it is possible to discern a number of youth commonly recruited to the action-set from the category for these activities. Those skinheads repeatedly recruited to form these action-sets comprise the quasi-group which provides a pool of available personnel from which future action-sets may be drawn. If there are several members constantly recruited to the action-set, one may characterize them as the core or clique of the quasi-group.

The quasi-group operates between the action-set and the category. It is larger than any single action-set for it contains those recruited on any one occasion plus those who will be recruited in the near future and those who have been recruited in the recent past. However, the quasi-group is also a subset of the category as not all skinheads in the category will be asked to join the same action-set. Therefore, within the total skinhead category there may be four or five quasi-groups consisting of perhaps six to ten members, linked by bridging weak ties. The number of personnel in the quasi-group depends on the length of a skinhead's involvement in the subculture. A prominent skinhead who has been involved in the subculture for several years and has thus built up his personal relationships will correspondingly have a larger pool of friends and acquaintances than a newcomer to the scene.

In an ideal sense, a skinhead could conceive of all others in the category 'skinhead' as members of his quasi-group, rather than reserving this label for those regularly recruited to the action-set. According to the skinhead ethos, skinheads aid each other in dangerous situations because of their categorical skinhead identity. In reality, the category 'skinhead' is divided into several quasi-groups. Assistance is not always offered unless a bridging tie exists between quasi-groups, and the identities are known. A prominent skinhead, such as Rhygin, has more chance of gaining assistance in a violent situation because he knows more people. Specifically, the task is often fighting, or at least the display of loyalty. More generally, one will often socialize with the same group of people who thus form one's immediate action-set. One recruits, or rather joins, one's action-set for a potential 'good night'. Therefore, the end product of Rhygin's shifts in membership of various action-sets is a very large quasi-group.

The total skinhead scene is framed within a larger English scene which, in turn, is a part of the Perth youth scene. The whole youth scene is an aggregation of many different sub-scenes which are brought together through those who participate in them. Interaction between members of these sub-scenes is sometimes violent but can also be of a more sociable nature. Internally, the skinhead scene is formed and re-formed as scenes become venues and venues scenes.

Scene and venue

In the same way that action-set relates to quasi-group, so venue relates to scene. 'Venue', as defined by *The Shorter Oxford English Dictionary* (1988, p. 2462), is the 'locality where an action is laid', 'the scene of a real or supposed action or event' or 'an appointed place of meeting'. 'Scene' is 'a view or picture presented to the eye (or to the mind) of a place, concourse, incident, series of actions or events, assemblage of objects, etc' (*The Shorter Oxford English Dictionary* 1988, p. 1900). In my discussion of the creation and maintenance of space, I wish to use scene and venue in strictly defined ways. Scenes are spatio-temporal domains. They are part of the day or nightlife of the city and their existence is established independently of those who frequent them. Venues are designated scenes patronized by known others at known or arranged times. In a sense, venues are owned. They belong to their patrons who create them by their presence.

Let me use an example to illustrate the difference between scene and venue. At point X in time there may be four scenes, A, B, C and D, spatio-temporally located in four different establishments that comprise the total skinhead scene. For the skinheads who frequent scene A, A is a venue, as it is a known locality frequented by other known personalities on a regular basis. To the other skinheads it remains a scene, an option available to them should they choose it but one which lacks their patronage. The total skinhead scene, at any one point in time, is the aggregate of these venues (as each scene will be a venue for some skinheads, otherwise it would not be a skinhead scene). Over a period of time a skinhead changes his patronage from one scene to another several times, sometimes with his action-set but sometimes alone. This switching of scene into venue and venue into scene (often accompanied by corresponding changes in the action-set), illustrated by Rhygin's career, makes the total scene dynamic.

There is a temporal aspect to the transformation of scene into venue and venue into scene. In the cycle of change from one venue to another, periods spent at one regular venue may become recognized times to be nostalgically reflected upon later. There is also recognition that a spatial move means a new beginning. Rhygin's verdict on the 'Ipswich Nights' (discussed in more detail in Chapter Eight) as 'the three best nights I think we've had' marked this period as an era, that is, a period of time marked by a distinctive character or mood. For a period to become categorized as an era by skinheads it would usually consist of 'good nights' (characterized by fighting, heavy drinking and possibly meetings with the opposite sex) and be located in a regular venue.

Eras may also centre around the activities of a particular quasi-group and therefore include several venues. The action-set might attend different venues each week, or on different nights of the week, but the period is still seen as an era because of the composition of the action-set or other common features. An era may include several regular venues at once, for example, one for Wednesday nights, one for Saturday nights and one for Sunday afternoons. Thus comments such as 'Remember the Ipswich [Hotel]' or 'They were really good [Sunday] sessions' (fondly remembered occasions at particular pubs) are common. These eras serve to map the immediate as well as the more distant past and become testaments to a skinhead's lengthy involvement in the subculture. Eras mark authenticity. In this respect, eras belong to the quasi-group whereas memories of particular incidents belong to the action-set. Therefore, connections lie between the shifts in scene to venue, and vice-versa, and the creation of eras for the quasi-group (because over a period of time more personnel are involved than just the action-set), and between good nights (i.e., particular incidents) and the action-set present on the said occasions.

A skinhead transforms his venue into a scene, by no longer attending (as long as other skinheads continue their patronage), or transforms a scene into his venue by choosing to attend over a period of time. This period may then become an era if enough events of subcultural significance take place, for example, fights with members of other subcultures, meetings with the opposite sex and/or heavy drinking.

The regular scenes the skinhead has available to choose from are mostly located in hotels, taverns, and nightclubs. Scenes can be relocated in other establishments for a number of reasons. A change of disc jockey may mean a change to music not favoured by skinheads or a changed management may alter dress standards and thus desired clientele. In some cases, there may have been fights with bouncers or members of other youth subcultures in past weeks. The establishment may be considered unsafe and avoided until the threat has subsided.

Scenes are spatio-temporally located within the inner city and suburbs. The various establishments which comprise the daytime skinhead scene differ from those offering entertainment at night. The daytime venues include several inner-city and some suburban hotels and taverns, some more up-market than others. There is a constant shifting of the predominant venue amongst these candidate scenes which again depends largely on managerial policies concerning access, even to the point of differing policies for different times during the day. In one pub, the manager agreed to serve skinheads before 12 noon, and between 2 p.m. and about 6 p.m., but not during the interim lunch or later evening periods. At this time, his preferred clientele, business people and restaurant and theatre-goers, patronized the bar. Outside these busy peaks, trade could be supplemented by the skinheads' attendance. In the evening, skinheads would usually attend one of their currently popular hotel scenes in the inner city. Skinheads preferring suburban venues followed a favourite band to its various engagements (this was a shifting venue). Should skinheads choose late-night entertainment, several nightclubs provided options from which to choose and again entry was governed by managerial policy. The set with whom I moved would attend in cycles, frequenting one club for a few weeks until there was inevitably trouble of one sort or another (to be fair, not always the fault of the skinheads) and entry was barred or the venue avoided. Another haunt would be sought until the same thing occurred. After several of these changes the first establishment may have relaxed its entry requirements and the cycle would begin again.

There are three types of venue in Perth. The English scene is located in regular venues where the bulk of personnel are to be found. The mixed scene, usually at a nightclub, occurs where there may be only a small number of skinheads present, but they know the club well (through patronage) and they know many of the other patrons. It is here that the interaction between members of sub-cultures (both within and outside the English scene) takes place. For the skinheads it is still a venue, despite them not being the majority group present, because they 'know it' rather than 'know about it'. This is the intermittent venue. The third type of venue is created by act of takeover. Here skinheads invade another scene, which is not one of their usual venues, to make it theirs for a short time. Takeovers are comparatively rare but one example is the exhibition football matches played between visiting British teams and a Western Australian representative side. Skinheads and other members of the English scene arrive in numbers at the sporting ground chosen for the fixture and make the ground their venue. This venue is of a temporary and unique nature.[5]

The ownership of venue

Regular venues are owned by skinheads, their regular patrons. In social action a territorial principle lies dormant until unusual circumstances accentuate differences. When American sailors flood Perth on Rest and Recreation Leave, their clothing, accents, haircuts and sometimes their behaviour will render them easily identifiable. On one occasion at a regular venue, anti-sailor sentiment assumed concrete form in a specific incident. A uniformed sailor had been moving through the throng and had accidentally spilt a drink held by a well-known ex-skinhead. The ex-skinhead's response was to grab the sailor by the lapels, head-butt him in the face and then push him away uttering a vicious 'Fuck off!' through clenched teeth. The sailors were seen by the skinheads (and the English scene members in general) as invading their regular venue, symbolically heralded in the disc jockey's playing of disco music for the visitors, and in the 'chatting-up' of the young women considered members of their general English scene and of this regular venue. The act of violence was thus a reflex of this scene.

This concept of venue ownership is germane to skinhead solidarity which is again dependent on social situations for its expression. In the regular venue, solidarity reflects the commonality of members of the English scene, but is not usually tested in situations because the risk of danger is slight due to this very commonality. However, within intermittent venues, threat can materialize easily. Out-numbered, skinheads realize a feeling of group solidarity (if only for the action-set present rather than for skinheads as a whole). Even the locating of one's group in a specific spatial position within the mixed-scene establishment can engender feelings of solidarity. Therefore, the ownership of venue and related group solidarity is framed situationally. It relates closely to the difference between scene and venue as, respectively, places invaded and where active differentiation occurs, and places owned and grounded in commonality.

Again, the spatio-temporal nature of the city scene plays a large part in determining situations for the demonstration of group solidarity. In the wider city scene where categorical relationships (Mitchell 1956) guide interaction and the frames in which interaction occurs, a skinhead rarely journeys into town at night without at least one friend. This rule is relaxed during the day and unaccompanied entry is common. The expression of solidarity is also dictated, in the broadest sense, by the temporal dimension of the city in the formation of what Hannerz (1980) calls traffic relationships, that is, relationships with strangers which involve minimal interaction (e.g., standing in a queue or opening a door).

The significance of skinhead groups

The outcome of the constant switching of scene to venue and venue to scene is the provision of access to the accumulation of 'good times', which can first be converted into memorialized events and then into social mileage. One's investment of time and energy yields happenings and the status which derives from participation in them. In the skinhead scheme, a person's standing is linked to personal performances. To attain the status of known identity one's performances must be both impressive and numerous. Collectively approved performances become social currency and this social currency is converted into one's social worth and esteem. From this currency a skinhead draws personal identity which is built on the common identity of 'skinhead' but then elaborated to include one's selective participation in scenes and venues.

The question of belonging or commonality is pertinent to this discussion. As I noted in Chapter One, Cohen (1982) outlines five elements which comprise belonging: commonality, a narrow range of relationships, idiom, trends of social organization, and locality. Skinhead patterns of association provide extensive information enabling the skinhead to map an ever-changing and potentially hostile environment.[6] However, these patterns, and therefore the skinhead subculture, are not grounded in locality, are not the product of inter-generational transmission, and are not the result of stable personnel. What then do they represent in terms of identification? What does a skinhead feel he is part of? The answer lies in commonality for the quasi-group (or scene), in being amongst other English youth. For the action-set (or venue), there is the belonging in, and identification with, a set of close consociates. The skinhead belongs to a recognizable way of doing things which appeals primarily to British youth who choose to follow an established subcultural tradition and to incorporate their ethnic origins into their personal identities during the teenage years.

Notes

1. For sociological discussions of 'gangs', see Bloch and Neiderhoffer (1958), Bordua (1961), Campbell (1984), Cloward and Ohlin (1960), A. K. Cohen (1955), the *Journal of Research into Crime and Delinquency*, 4(1), (1967), Miller (1958), Short (1968), and Thrasher (1927).

2. For a discussion of the Australian tradition of larrikinism, see Metcalfe (1985). Dunphy (1969) discusses 'cliques, crowds and

gangs' but his categories are static and the processural elements in his framework are aimed at individual development rather than at the group level.

3.   When a skinhead describes someone as a 'mate', he is usually referring to someone considered to be a close friend rather than the more egalitarian Australian usage in which the term may be used to greet a stranger.

4.   For Perth skinheads, calling one's self a 'rude boy' may have two quite distinct meanings: that the applicant has a knowledge of the history of postwar British subcultures, of reggae and of the West Indian nexus; or that he is modelling himself after the rude boys of The Specials era who, while supporting a band comprising several West Indians, saw no contradiction in also being racist.

5.   At the beginning of my fieldwork, Perth skinhead scenes were as follows: four hotels for drinking during the day, three hotels for drinking at night, and three nightclubs. The location of these scenes changed rapidly during the course of my fieldwork. At this time, only one of these (one of the hotels patronized at night) could be classed as a regular skinhead venue. The other licensed premises were mixed, intermittent venues.

6.   As do those of the African American streetcorner men described in *Soulside* (Hannerz 1969).

3 The meaning of visual style

The fascination for clothing as a semiotic signpost to the macro-sociological meaning of youth subcultures (namely, the class struggle) has prevented authors of works about English skinheads from exploring the relationship between the visual and performative aspects of style, and how these aspects combine to form the overall style of a social group. Hebdige (1982, pp. 27-28) describes skinhead visual style like this:

> The skinhead style, for all its apparent knuckleheadedness, is a consciously held pose, a deliberate turning back to earlier, more certain times when men were men and girls stuck by their blokes through thick and thin, a time when an observer could tell an individual's social status by merely glancing down at the footwear or at the way a person walked. Just watch the way a skinhead moves. The posture is organised as carefully as the length of the red tags or the Sta-prest or the hair. There is a lot of lapel twitching. The head twists out as if the skin is wearing an old fashioned collar that's too tight for comfort. The cigarette, tip turned in towards the palm, is brought down from the mouth in an exaggerated arc and held behind the back. It's a gesture reminiscent of barrack rooms and Borstals, of furtive smoking on parade. That's the dance of Skin. Compare it to the way a bobby pounds his beat or to the leisurely stroll Prince Philip adopts when he follows his wife on a walkabout. Both Prince and policeman, their hands clasped confidently behind their backs, move as if they own the world. Skinheads, on the other hand, are nervous and twitchy. They're always jumping out of the frame (...) They're always on their toes, ready to respond to the slightest provocation, ready to defend the little they possess (a football end, a pub, a street, a reputation). The dance of Skin

is, then, even for the girls, a mime of awkward masculinity – the geometry of menace. For skinheads are playing with the only power at their disposal – the power of having nothing (much) to lose. The style, in other words, *fits*.

This evocative quotation tells us little about the skinhead's own perception of his visual style nor does it give any clues about the performative dimensions of style. What does visual style mean to a skinhead and what is its significance for the social interaction of everyday life?

The visual component of style is the centre of a skinhead's cultural world. It is the pivot around which he organizes his finances and identity, and the concept through which he categorizes social types. Visual style provides the grammar of everyday interaction for the members of these groups. In place of formalized structure, skinheads use visual style to organize their relationships, to recognize friend and foe, to categorize social types, and to signal their belonging. Visual style is more than a set of clothes to be discarded at will, rather an attitude to life given expression in apparel and behaviour. The wearing of skinhead visual style is the sign for the announcement of a categorical opposition to the mainstream world.

A contrastive account of the differences between the English and Perth skinhead's visual style provides supporting evidence for my choice of an ethnicity-oriented approach to skinheads in Western Australia.

English skinhead visual style

An extraordinarily detailed account of the evolution of English skinhead clothing style for the period 1968-71 is provided by Ferguson (1982).[1] Other authors have listed the standard dress but not dealt with variations and changes over time (e.g., Brake 1974, Hebdige 1979). Although Ferguson's account lacks the performative details of style, he provides an excellent pictorial description of English skinhead clothing (see pages 37–40) accompanied by explanatory text. For present purposes I will summarize Ferguson's account, adopting his division of clothing into categories.

Coats

Apparently any coat passed muster in 1968, the early period of development of the skinhead visual style. Thus army, donkey, denim, leather, corduroy, suede, or Harrington jackets were all acceptable, as were parkas and anoraks. At the top of the heap was the

1968-9

Donkey jacket
Union shirt
Clip ons
Blue jeans

Levi's two piece
T-shirt
Air Wair

Football scarf worn in the
conventional mode
British army two-piece
NCB boots, white steel

Ben Sherman, button-down collar
The mac
Jeans
Bouncing soles, etc..
Sheepskin

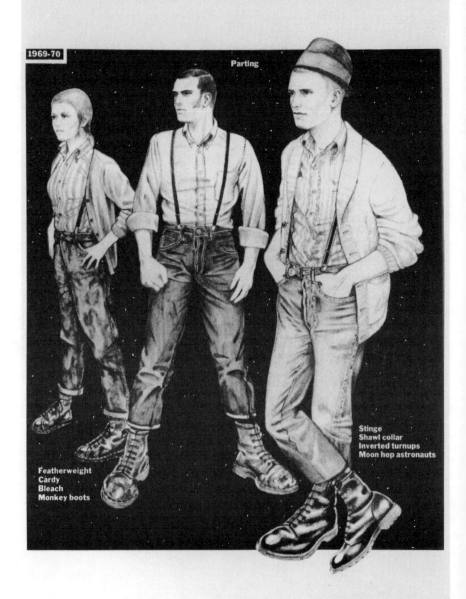

1969-70

Parting

Featherweight
Cardy
Bleach
Monkey boots

Stinge
Shawl collar
Inverted turnups
Moon hop astronauts

1970

Shetland V-neck
Patch
Air Wair shoes

Navy Sherman
Fawn suit
Oxblood
Cordovan
Wing tip
Brogues

Jaytex
Sta-Prest
Smooth leather uppers

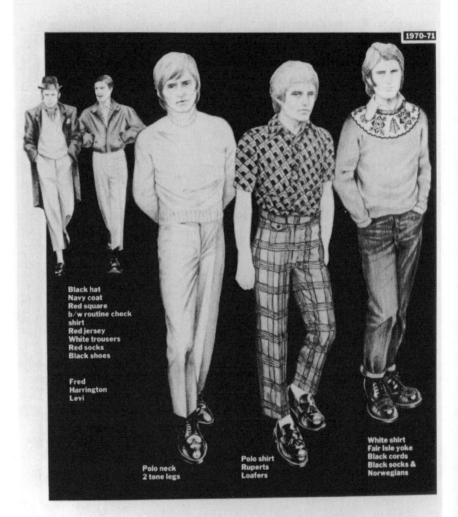

1970-71

Black hat
Navy coat
Red square
b/w routine check
shirt
Red jersey
White trousers
Red socks
Black shoes

Fred
Harrington
Levi

Polo neck
2 tone legs

Polo shirt
Ruperts
Loafers

White shirt
Fair Isle yoke
Black cords
Black socks &
Norwegians

sheepskin coat. Ferguson claims that this was the ultimate skinhead coat and could be worn with pride anywhere between 1968 and 1971. The crombie coat, however, came to prominence after skinheads had worked a drastic stylistic evolution with the onset of the 'smooth' look in 1971.

Hats

Football club hats and scarves were worn, and the 'pork-pie' trilby enjoyed spells as a popular accessory.

Hair

Prior to the blossoming of skinhead styles, hair was already worn very short by the majority of men, but the length shortened to a uniform one-quarter of an inch all over. Although baldness was not fashionable, very close-cropped hair was, hence the name 'skinhead'. Some of the variations on this 'iron-filing length hair' were merging the hair at the back of the head into the neck, a squared-off back or 'Boston', or rounded at the back. Sideboards also became popular at one time. For females, hair was initially worn in ordinary styles with skinhead clothes. Later, females adopted the male crop but with a longer fringe.

Suit jackets

Suit jackets were worn single-breasted with three, and sometimes four or five, buttons worn high. The lapels were very narrow but the pocket flaps gradually increased in size. The jacket was also narrow-shouldered, high, had a tight waist and was flared over the hips.

Trousers

Trousers, in the first instance, were basic 'parallels' (with clip-on braces) with variations on seams, pleats and turn-ups. Between 1968 and 1971 the leg width increased from eighteen to twenty inches. After 1971, 'baggies' arrived. For suits, mohair was the favourite choice, first in dark colours but later in check, houndstooth and two-tone patterns.

Jeans

Levi's were most popular in London whereas Wrangler dominated skinhead sales in the Midlands and North by 1970. The Levi's had zips but the others (including Lee Rider) had button-up flies. The jeans were worn straight-leg, rolled-up or cut-off at the required length, and were often bleached. Army pants were also common initially. Levi's were the makers of the hallowed Sta-Prest, any colour being acceptable. Cords were worn only sparingly until mid 1971 when black, bottle-green, and navy, straight-leg Levi cords became increasingly popular.

Shirts

To begin with any shirt that was not fashionable was acceptable, to be followed by the early Ben Shermans with their low-set second button so that the collar sat open. Later, the makers of the Ben Sherman were to follow other manufacturers and lift the button. Usual colours were white and pastel shades before stripes (varying in colour and width) were introduced. Later, weaves and checks were favoured. The button-down style was superseded by the rounded 'beagle' collar in all colours and checks. The Fred Perry shirt again became prominent in the summer of 1971.

Ties

Ties could be regimental, football or other club, or old school with the occasional polka-dot, but usually in more restrained patterns and colours.

Boots and shoes

Initially boots with concealed steel toe-caps and heels were popular, but after such boots were declared to be offensive weapons when worn at football matches their popularity subsided. The capped boot made way for the Doc Marten. Eight-eyelet Air Wear brown was by far the most popular boot. They were polished in cherry-red, brown, tan or red, with black smeared into the creases of each boot to remove the taint of newness. Black Doc Martens did not become popular until 1970. 'Eleven-eyelets' were also worn but these did not come with the prized Doc Marten heel tag. Doc Marten shoes were seen mostly on younger teenagers. For the females, 'monkey boots' were the norm as the manufacturers of Doc Marten did not make small sizes. When small sizes began being produced, females also began wearing Doc Marten boots. In 1970 the American brogue (black-grained or tan) was worn, as were 'smoothies' which were identical to brogues except for the smooth, non-grained finish. Both these and the slip-on loafer were made by Faith Royal and brogues were known as 'Royals'. The loafers, still made by Faith Royal, continued to be popular and were modified so as to be lighter than brogues and were provided with an all-round sole extension. Towards the end of the era of the 'pure' skinhead style (late 1971) heavy, lace-up 'Norwegians' with large toes were worn. This style's heel eventually grew into the 'platforms' of mid to late 1972. With the advent of 'glamrock' some innovative youth wore brightly painted Doc Martens.

Therefore, as Knight (1982, p. 10) observes, 'The mods' fanatical eye for detail became an important element in the skinhead style'. English skinheads were susceptible to fashion in that clothing styles changed radically and arbitrarily over the relatively short period of three years, possibly as a response to a subcultural system which encouraged clothing trendsetters. These trends would subsequently be taken up by other skinheads. The rapid change in the visual style of English skinheads was a response to internal factors generated by the subculture – the need to stay ahead of the crowd. English skinhead visual style conforms to Barthes's (1983) notion of 'fashion' in the constant and arbitrary changing of items.

Perth skinhead visual style

Following Ferguson's categories, Perth skinhead clothing can be described as follows.

Coats

While essential for English skinhead visual style, coats are not an essential part of Perth visual style because of Perth's warm climate. The ubiquitous denim jacket (usually Levi's or Wrangler) is owned by most skinheads and the black Harrington jacket is also common. The crombie is seen as the top skinhead coat and is to be worn with pride, drawing admiration from other skinheads. The airforce flight jacket is popular, usually green but sometimes blue. Leather jackets are sometimes worn.

Hats

The hat plays no significant role in the visual style of Perth skinheads except for the very rare pork-pie (rude boy) hat and occasional flat-cap, traditionally worn by the English working-class male.

Hair

The length of the crop depends on the particular skinhead's favoured activities. As I explain later, 'day' skinheads tend to wear a 'Number One' or 'Two' while those wishing to gain entry into pubs and clubs settle for a 'Number Three 3' or 'Four' or 'flat-tops' (short on the sides like the crop but with a longer fringe worn up to create the flat look on top of the head). The number of the haircut denotes the setting on the barber's electric razor, with 'One' being the shortest and 'Four' the longest. I never saw beards nor moustaches.[2]

Suit jackets

Like coats, suit jackets are relatively rare even at night, although some stylistically knowledgeable skinheads possessed two-tone (Tonik) jackets. In Perth, suit jackets and trousers comprise part of the mod look and are usually scorned accordingly.

Trousers

Although more popular than suit jackets, trousers still rate a poor second to jeans. Trousers are usually worn at night with the Sta-Prest brand favoured, as well as other tapered styles. If trousers are worn, they are never flared and it is common for old pairs of straight-leg trousers to be tailored into a tightly-tapered style. If worn with boots, the trousers are often shorter than normal to display the boots to full advantage. Only once did I see a pair of parallels (also sometimes known as 'bags' after the 'Oxford bags') which were common up to 1980.

Jeans

Any brand of jeans can be worn as long as they are straight-legged. Favoured brands include Levi's, Wrangler, and Lee. Jeans may also be bleached and worn shorter on the leg, about mid-shin, to show off the Doc Marten boots.

Shirts

The ultimate shirt is an original Ben Sherman with a three-button collar and stitched pleat in the back. They correspond to the earlier English Ben Shermans where the second button was set low causing the collar to sit open. However, more recently manufactured Ben Shermans will suffice, where the pleat is not stitched. The Fred Perry sports-shirt, bearing the laurel leaves crest, is very popular even though it is also worn by mods. Other sports-shirts of similar style but different brand are acceptable, for example, Puma, Adidas, Penguin, and so on. T-shirts are usually only worn during the day and bear pro-English motifs such as football teams and the names of 'Oi!' music bands. (Oi! is a brand of music favoured by skinheads – a fast, aggressive, uncomplicated sound played by bands such as The 4 Skins, Cockney Rejects and Skrewdriver).

Ties

Because ties are associated with mods they are rarely worn by Perth skinheads. In fact, I do not recall seeing a skinhead wearing a tie, unless consciously dressing 'moddy' for some reason (e.g., to gain entry to a nightclub).

Boots and shoes

The full range of 'Docs' or Doc Marten boots is worn including black eleven-holers, eight-holers, 'steelies', Airwear and Astronauts, all variations of the same basic boot. Black boots are most popular but some skinheads also own an oxblood-coloured pair. Other acceptable footwear includes brogues and black Doc Marten shoes. Oxblood Doc Marten shoes are usually worn by mods and 'trendies' and are therefore rejected by Perth skinheads.

Jumpers and cardigans

An addition to Ferguson's categories is that of jumpers and cardigans. Because of Perth's warm climate, coats are rarely worn with a corresponding change in emphasis to jumpers and cardigans. The Fred Perry brand is again desirable along with those made by Pringle, but ordinary brands are acceptable. The style is V-neck and made from a light wool rather than thicker, heavier types. Sleeveless jumpers are sometimes worn.

The visual style I have described was common for several years prior to my fieldwork (late 1970s through to 1983) and during the fieldwork and initial writing period (1984-8). A Perth skinhead in 1990 could have worn the same, or a very similar, outfit to the one worn in 1985 or 1980 and still be recognized as a skinhead, both by the general public and by other skinheads

Despite the differences in visual style between English and Perth skinheads, Perth skinheads look to their idealized 'home', England, for inspiration. Clothing obtained in England and brought back to Perth has created a grey market. Almost anything bought in England, especially from such shops as The Last Resort, a retail establishment set up in London by some enterprising skinheads and specializing in clothing and other skinhead paraphernalia, can fetch as much as twice the price of similar articles on sale in Perth. As Nutter once retorted, after being criticized by another skinhead for wearing a leather coat of a type not usually worn, 'This is what all the skinheads are wearing in England now, mate!' This silenced the would-be arbiter of visual style. Some skinhead clothing items are unavailable in Perth, these items only being available from England. Even if skinhead items are available in Perth, products purchased in England are more desirable because they are proof of one's continuing links with 'home'. The knowledgeable skinhead is aware of English clothing trends and acquires as many authentic items as possible by making personal trips to England. Alternatively, travelling friends or relatives may return from trips laden with English-made clothing items.

Ethnicity and visual style

The differences in clothing styles between English and Perth skinheads can be traced to the experience of immigration. With the exportation of the total skinhead style, the working-class base of the English skinhead subculture became less important than the ethnic dimension. Whereas the English skinhead was concerned primarily with demonstrating his membership of the working class first and his English ethnicity second (Hebdige 1982, pp.28-35), in Perth this trend is reversed and ethnicity takes precedence.[3] The Perth skinhead is framed within a larger English youth scene, the members of which look to England for inspiration. This scene has become increasingly attractive to English youth regardless of socioeconomic position since the dynamism of Punk in the late 1970s, and the resulting profusion of musical and dress styles. Perth skinheads also have little performative knowledge of the skinhead scene in England. Therefore, starting with a generalized idea of clothing style, the Perth type is produced. Consequently, Perth skinheads exhibit more chronological latitude in the range of permissible styles. Still central are the standard Doc Marten boots, straight-leg jeans, T-shirts emblazoned with pro-England motifs, and the aggressively short crop. But alongside these standard items are those shared with other youth groups originating in England such as mods. For example, both the Perth skinhead and the Perth mod are equally comfortable wearing a Fred Perry sports-shirt or a flat-top hairstyle.

That Perth skinheads are most interested in signalling their English ethnicity is further supported by an examination of the wider English scene. After ceasing to be a skinhead, the English lad will, along with many of his age grade, either become a mod or move into the 'ex-skin' category, known identities who no longer wear skinhead clothing but who retain other features of the total skinhead style, for example, fighting and the frequenting of skinhead scenes. These ex-skins are still very much a part of the English scene, comprising an upper level of older members who have progressed through the skinhead stage to become known identities.[4] Typical dress for these ex-skins includes tassled slip-on shoes, button-down collar shirts, trousers, and slightly longer hair, usually with a fringe. The style softens, perhaps best represented by the changing of the ultimate skinhead trait – the growing of the crop. As Ace once remarked to Rhygin, 'It's good to see you growing your hair, you're getting too old for all this'. In some cases the ex-skin can become somewhat invisible stylistically, unlike those who choose the mod option. He may dress 'like a trendy' but is still known to others in the larger network. Tales of past exploits can guarantee recognition by younger skinheads, 'If you're studying skinheads you should talk to Zeus. He used to be one of Perth's top skinheads.' This process usually only applies to those who have remained skinheads for a large part of their stylistic career. Some leave the style earlier before they establish reputations as skinheads and become members of other flamboyant youth styles, such as the teddy boy.

Visits to Perth by British football teams provide another opportunity to examine the precedence of ethnicity. No matter what one is stylistically when the visiting team plays, perhaps a mod or an ex-skinhead (if not 'out of it' for too long), for that afternoon you are once again a skinhead. Out come the old boots, braces, bleached jeans (or, if you are older, the parallels), and various scarves. It does not matter if one does not ordinarily support the visiting team. Internal divisions between team loyalties are superseded by the unity symbolized in 'our' team, the visiting British side, versus 'them', the Western Australian representative side. At the match, the chants begin, 'If you all hate coppers, clap your hands!' and skinheads attempt to recreate the atmosphere of a British football terrace. Consequently, reported skinhead numbers for these games are always inflated by an undiscriminating press. This reverting to skinhead identity also occurred at a notorious Madness concert, with many ex-skinheads and mods once again donning their Doc Marten boots to be reported by the local papers as 'skinheads'.[5]

A further complication is that England experienced what Cashmore called 'the second coming' of skinheads (1984, p. 63), a more politically-oriented version clearly influenced by the anarchism and nihilism of Punk, with corresponding alterations in clothing style. Unfortunately, there is a dearth of material as to what this change meant performatively. At the time of my field research, this later style had not yet filtered through to Perth, one of the reasons being that the Australian government has reduced quotas for British migrants in recent years, and so there are not as many English youth arriving in Perth. Another reason is that the British social conditions producing this second coming are markedly different to those existing in Perth.

As a consequence of this focus on the announcement of English ethnicity, the Perth skinhead is virtually free to draw on any of the multitude of stylistic changes that have occurred in England, precisely because these items are seen to signal Englishness. English skinhead style has evolved through many sequential developments covering various brands of jackets, shoes, and other clothing items. In Perth, skinheads may combine different clothing items that in England were worn at different periods in the evolution of a distinct visual style. This is not to imply that there are no fads in Perth skinhead style in which a clothing item (or items) becomes more common or desirable. Rather, what is currently popular in Perth does not always correspond to what was, or is, currently popular in England.

Perth skinheads are not somehow less stylish than their English counterparts, lacking in stylistic integrity, or stylistically backward because their visual style has changed only slowly. They are responding to a different set of circumstances and their response is shaped by ethnic rather than class affiliation. The Perth skinhead is interested in signalling his ethnicity in the public context of urban arenas. His response is to factors external to the group which relate to the urban lifestyle – the creation of meaning and personal and categorical identity.

Spheres of style

The main regulator of visual style in Perth is the activity at hand. Spending an afternoon in a suburban pub is very different from a Friday night 'in town' (in central Perth). Spending the afternoon in an inner-city pub is different again from spending it in a suburban hotel. These differences lead me to a discussion of spheres of style. Within the skinhead subculture, there are two main styles corresponding to chosen activities. I have termed these two main sets of activity 'day' and 'night' style. They consist of different activities but also apply to different groups of skinheads who favour particular modes of activity. 'Day' activities differ from 'night' activities and this difference is expressed conspicuously in dress and attitude.

Day style

The skinheads opting for day style spend much of their time in town. They are usually unemployed, or sporadically employed, and rarely visit the music-oriented pubs and clubs. Their nights are spent walking around town, going to parties (sometimes invited, sometimes not), or drinking in public bars. Days in town involve a constant relationship with the general public. Thus the visual style is unapologetically aggressive and involves being 'booted-up' (fully dressed complete with boots) in the traditional skinhead uniform of Doc Marten boots, rolled-up jeans, pro-British T-shirt, and perhaps a denim or flight-jacket. This group wear a selected version of the British visual style dispensing with the spectrum of combinations to be left with a basic look that starts with the obligatory boots and short crop. The hair is usually worn in a Number Two or Three with the occasional Number One or Four. I think it significant that quite a number of skinheads have their hair cut at establishments in the city so as to be seen freshly shorn and therefore further announce their skinhead identity fresh from the barber's chair. The day visual style is drawn from any of the following items. Doc Marten boots are worn, usually black (but occasionally cherry-red) and less often black brogues or black Doc Marten shoes. Jeans, straight-leg and sometimes bleached, are worn above the boots, or 'army greens' or Sta-Prest trousers. These are complemented by a T-shirt or by the infrequent Fred Perry sports-shirt (which is normally saved for the evening) or other less status-laden brands such as those manufactured by Penguin, Puma, or Adidas. Completing the day look is the denim jacket (Levi or Wrangler) or airforce flight-jacket.

To facilitate the creation of this generalized public relationship much time would be spent 'in the mall' (the pedestrian shopping mall in the heart of central Perth), standing or sitting around talking, joking, making fun of passers-by, and seeing 'who else was in town' (skinheads or others). For some skinheads it also meant mixing with other in-town youths who were not necessarily skinheads. I once saw a well-known skinhead speaking amiably with a male and female in their mid-teens who would, by any skinhead's standards, be categorized as 'bogs' (i.e., they were wearing predominantly black clothing, had very long hair, wore black desert boots [known colloquially as 'DB's'], and were of Australian, Italian or Aboriginal origin). They knew one another's names and parted on friendly terms. Rhygin's categorical response to me later was that he would 'never talk to bogs'. This sort of camaraderie with other daytime inhabitants of the inner city seemed fairly common for some skinheads, if not usual. One group of skinheads, including the skinhead mentioned above, drinks at a particular hotel with two punk males, two punk females, and a rockabilly. Walking through town this group also stops and talks to other members of youth subcultures. The ethic of categorical opposition to other subcultures may be mediated by common experience – being young, unemployed, in town, and bored. I attribute Rhygin's opposition to this fraternization with the 'enemy' to his less frequent presence, and therefore common experience, in town.

Night style

The skinheads with whom I moved preferred the nightlife of Perth and wore a clothing style more suited to this chosen activity. While still occasionally spending a day in town and knowing many members of the day style to which I have referred, they dressed in a smarter, less antagonistic style. Often they had been day skinheads themselves at some earlier stage and still occasionally mixed with the day skinheads. Dressing in a less aggressive clothing style facilitates easier access to nightclubs which are sometimes loath to include skinheads in their clientele. As one skinhead said, 'You have to look like a mod to get into nightclubs'. Impersonating mods is seen as unacceptable by day skinheads who are unwilling to forsake their stylistic integrity for nightclub entry. However, those who do choose the night option are not thought of as lesser skinheads. Some of the day skinheads are barred from entry into some of the pubs and clubs because of past 'trouble'.

The clothing pool from which various combinations of the night style are drawn consists mainly of the following items. Instead of Doc Marten boots, which prevent access to most evening venues, black Doc Marten shoes or brogues are worn. The socks 'must' (as Rhygin informed me) be white or red. Trousers should ideally be Sta-Prest though tapered pants suffice, and jeans should also be narrow, preferably straight-legged. The smart night skinhead wears a Fred Perry sports-shirt or a button-down, original Ben Sherman shirt with stitched pleat in the back, another similar brand of dress shirt, or a sports-shirt such as a Penguin (made by an Australian company, Bonds). Such is the emphasis on the Fred Perry shirt that I had one skinhead, Ace, pull my jumper open to check if my sports-shirt was a 'Perry'. On discovering that it was a Penguin, he commented with a smile, 'Oh, it's only a Fred Penguin'. To complement the Fred Perry sports-shirt, a Perry jumper or cardigan is favoured, but again other brands are acceptable. Alternatively, a Harrington, denim, leather, or flight-jacket might be worn over the shirt or jumper. Finally, hair is usually worn in a Number Four or a flat-top by the skinheads favouring the night option as this presents a less aggressive look to facilitate entry into entertainment venues.

Although many of the items worn in day and night styles are similar, it is the co-ordination of clothing that separates the styles. A major difference is that Doc Marten boots are not worn at night if a skinhead wishes to attend a nightclub or a music-oriented pub. For night wear, a skinhead might wear brogues, trousers, a Fred Perry sports-shirt, and a denim jacket. If the same skinhead had gone out that day he might have worn Doc Marten boots, bleached jeans, a Union Jack T-shirt, and a flight-jacket, and thus presented quite a different front. In many ways, night style is a smartened version of the day style, altered to meet the exigencies of night activity – entering nightclubs, 'getting off with' (picking up) young women, and generally looking 'smart'. There are drawbacks though. Because the possibility of serious fights increases at night so does the risk of damage to expensive clothes. One Friday night, when Rhygin was aware there could be 'trouble', he wore his 'least-favourite' Fred Perry sports-shirt and trousers in case the threat materialized.

While some skinheads only participate in one of the two available styles, there are others who move between these two styles, equally accepted and at home in both. Movement from day style to night style often, but not always, corresponds to the maturation of a skinhead. As he gets older and is admitted freely onto licensed premises, the night style may appeal more with its seductive promise of drinking, fighting, and women. Before this maturation, satisfaction may be gained from just being in town with other skinheads and announcing newly-claimed skinhead identity to the public. Alternatively, the skinhead may prefer day style or be prevented from participating in night activity because of exclusion from entertainment venues. Some skinheads are equally comfortable participating in either style. They may frequently visit inner-city pubs to drink with skinheads who favour day style. However, they might also frequent the night skinhead's regular and mixed venues and this change in activity is signalled in the changing of visual style.

In some ways, the split between day and night style is a misnomer because skinheads sometimes wear what I have termed day clothing at night. If skinheads attend a venue which does not require alteration of visual style for entry (e.g., the exchanging of brogues for boots) then they will often wear the day style. The difference between day and night style is attitude, which is reflected in clothing, rather than temporal considerations. I chose 'day' and 'night' because these terms reflect the difference of emphasis between activity usually requiring the less obviously aggressive clothing style (night) and those activities where dress requirements are less rigid and allow the 'booted-up' style (day) to be worn.

Personality style

The movement of skinheads between day and night style raises the issue of personality and the consequences for interaction. Social relationships among Perth skinheads are labile. When studying a social aggregation of this type, one unintended but perhaps unavoidable consequence is to present a picture of a more formalized and rigid system than actually exists. Limits on dress styles, opinions of people of other races and ethnicities, and attitudes to the opposite sex appear fixed when, in reality, some members of the subculture may not necessarily share a particular view. In the skinhead subculture one can hold almost any belief, even running contradictory to a general skinhead view, provided one will back this view up, if necessary, with force.

Generalized shared understandings exist about activities such as fighting, loyalty to friends, drinking, and relations with the opposite sex and with the police. But skinheads conform to these understandings in varying degrees and may hold unusual views on other matters. For example, one night in a pub, George argued with Pete about Pete's sympathetic view of the Rastafarian movement, an unusual sympathy for a skinhead. After a heated altercation followed by a tense moment of visual confrontation, George turned and stormed off. He returned later to apologize to Pete, excusing his behaviour by explaining that he'd split-up with his long-term girlfriend earlier in the evening. Despite his own physical inferiority and George's acknowledged 'hardness', Pete was prepared to fight to defend his view. Subsequently, whenever Pete was being insulted or stirred by other skinheads and George was present, George would invariably interject with, 'You leave my little Rasta mate alone!'

The creation of personality is reflected in visual style. Pete sympathizes with the Rastafarian cult and sometimes wears T-shirts featuring the Rastafarian colours of gold, green and red. While this item announces a belief not common to the skinhead subculture, Pete is still accepted as a skinhead by other skinheads such as George. Doc Marten boots and the crop are basic to the skinhead uniform but between these two items a skinhead may express his own particular personality. Skinheads may wear English football club shirts expressing their ethnicity and regional affiliation within this ethnicity. Tattoos often feature pro-English motifs. Different skinheads wear a variety of such items of clothing and tattoos which thus express their personality while at the same time wearing items which signal their categorical skinhead identity.

The personal expression displayed by various clothing items is not limited to ethnicity or region. Night skinheads may be judged as 'smart' if they combine elements of the skinhead night style in an approved manner. The knowledgeable night skinhead expresses his knowledge of subcultural diacritics through clothing. This desirable attribute formed the basis for a 'dressing-up' competition between Rhygin and Ace, arranged one Saturday evening. The challenge was to see who could look the 'smartest'. The two competitors arrived the following week at a pre-arranged suburban hotel dressed in their finery. The bar attendant asked to decide the winner diplomatically declared a draw. Rhygin later confessed to me his opinion that Ace should have won, but the competition was as much about entertainment as anything else.

Emphasis on smartness is more applicable to clothing worn at night and to the skinheads who favour night activity because at night the clothing-conscious skinhead may exhibit the full range of sartorial elegance. Instead of developing an argot, skinheads express themselves through a language of presentation towards the world which encompasses not only the correct subcultural clothing but also the right combination of these clothing items to present an approved stylistic appearance. Thus a comment such as, 'He looks smart' (usually followed by 'but don't tell him that') carries the implicit approval of the items selected and their combination. Visual style has a physical dimension in that the presentation of an approved clothing combination will be more successful if the skinhead is of impressive physical dimensions, or at least not overweight. One's physical appearance and expression of an air of confidence combine to enhance clothing and its presentation. The comment 'he looks smart, but don't tell him that' demonstrates that while tacit approval may be given for smart dress, compliments are not usually offered. This reluctance stems from a status-conscious ethos that precludes openly awarding social credit to others, and from the skinhead emphasis on performance in modes of activity patterned by the subculture. A skinhead may be 'smart' but if he does not perform satisfactorily in these activities, the label 'skinhead' may no longer be accorded him by other skinheads.

However, even dressing in an approved way does not necessarily guarantee the newcomer acceptance. Standing with a group of skinheads at a football match, Nutter and Roy both tried to hassle me for money. Their manner was superficially friendly but with the underlying menace that sometimes characterizes skinhead inter-action, a sort of aggressive sociability. I stood firm and said I did not have any to spare, just enough to buy myself a few drinks. They turned to Chris who was dressed in black boots, bleached jeans, red T-shirt, and sunglasses. His aim was to look like the archetypal rude boy. Even though Chris was dressed in a skinhead clothing style (Rhygin told me later that Chris had bought the 'wrong type of boots' but he was certainly much closer to the others in dress than I), Roy and Nutter chose to ridicule him, relishing in his obvious discomfort. Roy leant over and used the steel splint on a recently-cut finger to slash the toe of one of Chris's brand new boots. He then stood back awaiting Chris's reaction. Chris chose to leave the gathering and stood some thirty yards away with his girlfriend, who was standing with another young woman. The remaining skinheads found the incident humorous.

Roy and Nutter had first tried to pressure me into buying them drinks and had tried to use me as the butt of their jokes. They soon realized that Chris, despite being dressed in a more appropriate style than I, could more easily be intimidated, and they acted on this perceived weakness. Chris was not harassed solely because he had bought the wrong type of boots. Rhygin mentioned this privately to me later, but neither Nutter nor Roy made any similar comment, although the slashing of the boot may have been a more non-verbal statement of their disapproval. A second point, which Rhygin noted, was that I made no claim to be a skinhead whereas Chris, perhaps to cover nervousness as he was a relative newcomer to the group, appeared somewhat over-confident about his supposed rude boy/skinhead status. Nutter and Roy, affronted by his pretensions, soon cured him of this illusion.

To become a skinhead is not to enter a closed system that forces the newcomer to adopt certain attitudes and dress. On the contrary, there is a high emphasis placed on individuality within the basic skinhead identity signalled by Doc Marten boots and crop. Should a newcomer to the scene be overly compliant he will be exploited as someone who can easily be taken advantage of and probably shunned thereafter. If the novice is sufficiently assertive he will be able to slot into the network easily. This point relates closely to the notion of 'self-liquidating positions and identity' (Sansom 1981) in that skinheads forge their own positions within the subculture through personality. When a skinhead leaves the immediate scene, the position he has created disappears with him; it is not a formalized niche awaiting the arrival of a new incumbent. Each newcomer must forge his own position.

The ownership of visual style

One Saturday night, Rhygin, Chris, Dennis, Carol, Susan and I visited a pub featuring a band favoured by skinheads. The mood of the visit was fairly relaxed with drinking, dancing and talking being the main activities. About 11 p.m., Rhygin saw a lad wearing long hair, running shoes, and a T-shirt featuring an Oi! music motif. Rhygin took umbrage at this stylistic combination claiming that someone with hair 'that long' and wearing running shoes should not wear such a T-shirt. According to Rhygin, Oi! music was skinhead property. When the stylistic offender left the dance floor, Rhygin shouted to him and the lad approached our table. The following exchange took place:

> Rhygin (in disgust): 'Where are you from then?' (to ascertain if the youth was of English birth).
> T-shirt wearer: 'What does it matter?'
> Rhygin: 'It matters to me!' (as T-shirt wearer turns and walks away).
> Rhygin (yelling): 'Trendy fucking bastard!'

Hearing this last comment, the T-shirt wearer half-turned towards Rhygin and raised his middle finger in a derogatory gesture. This incensed Rhygin who got up and strode purposefully over to the other's table, whereupon a scuffle ensued.

In this incident Rhygin is exerting what he considered to be skinhead control over items deemed to belong to skinheads. The offender is clearly not a skinhead, as is demonstrated by his hairstyle and footwear, and is not claiming skinhead identity. But for Rhygin, Oi! music is skinhead music and for this reason the shirt was 'owned' by skinheads. Here is a person who is clearly not a skinhead announcing his liking for skinhead music. Rhygin regarded the T-shirt as skinhead property in the public scene. He therefore felt that he should take the appropriate steps to rectify the 'theft' of skinhead property.[6]

Another aspect of the ownership of visual style is provided by the case of Smithy who, by consensus, was now 'out-of-it' (had ceased to be a skinhead) but would still 'boot-up' (dress in skinhead clothing, especially Doc Marten boots) when attending certain events. On one occasion, we had been at a suburban pub for the afternoon and the lads had decided to continue the evening at a local haunt patronized by skinheads. Smithy went home to change his clothing and returned resplendent in rolled-up jeans and shiny black boots. The others accused him openly of only wearing his boots 'with the lads' and also discussed his wearing of skinhead uniform at length later. A few months later, Nutter left for England. Relatives, many skinheads and other friends came to the airport to see him off. A day at the airport is seen by skinheads as something of a carnival. The Union Jack hangs brightly and instantly recognizable in the corner of the bar. The airport provides a chance to be seen by the public on a large scale – to announce ethnicity and, through this, identity. Socially, the airport meeting is a chance to find out what people 'have been up to' recently and to congregate in an alcoholic farewell for mates. Smithy turned up in boots, bleached jeans, and a Ben Sherman shirt. His dress was again commented on by several skinheads who said that he was 'booting-up' only for this special occasion while dressing like a trendy at other times.

The comments made on Smithy's behaviour by other skinheads show the relationship between visual and performative style. Smithy entered public scenes, the pub and the airport, dressed as a skinhead and thus established his relationship with the general public as a skinhead. However, in past months he had failed to fulfil the necessary requirements for the privilege of wearing the skinhead uniform. He no longer went into town with other skinheads, preferring the company of a female partner. To wear skinhead clothing and to be accorded skinhead identity, the applicant for this identity must invest leisure time with other skinheads. This aspect of visual style is also pertinent to the next example.

The third case concerns the amount of time spent in town, an integral part of being a skinhead. Whether this time be in the evening or day is not so important. Being in town effectively means being with other skinheads. Nutter was telling Rhygin and Ace of a possible invitation to a skinhead barbecue. The skinhead host was called Joe and when asked where Joe lived, Nutter replied, 'Somewhere in the hills'. He also said that Joe 'never' came into town any more and added mockingly, 'He's a country skin'. Again, in Nutter's judgement of Joe, we witness the difference between claiming skinhead identity and being accorded that identity by other skinheads. Like Smithy, Joe has not spent time 'with the lads' and has therefore failed in his quest for 'skinhead' status.

These incidents highlight the skinhead ownership of visual style. To call oneself a skinhead, and more importantly to be acknowledged as a skinhead by other skinheads, one must perform satisfactorily in terms of the investment of both time and performance. These examples thus show that skinhead authenticity has two essential components: the correct visual presentation of the self and satisfactory performance in subcultural modes of action. The skinheads were objecting to Smithy's wearing of skinhead clothing while not participating in skinhead activity. He was presenting himself as a skinhead to the undiscriminating public without continuing to earn the necessary qualifications through the investment of time. (He had done so in the past; there was no question of him not having been a skinhead.) Thus, while the public may categorize Smithy, Joe, and the Oi! T-shirt wearer as skinheads, the possessors of knowledge, the skinheads themselves, object to the theft of their visual style by those lacking personal commitment.

We can therefore set up a three-way model of judgement which revolves around knowledge of style and its ownership:

1   There is visual style which establishes the relationship between skinheads and the general public, who possess a basic knowledge of the visual component of style but not of the performative.

2   There is public participation which belongs to the scenes where skinheads and the on-scene public interact (e.g., other youth, police, bar owners).

3   There are the skinheads themselves who possess detailed knowledge of both the visual and the performative aspects which make up their style.

Skinheads, often denied access to material status or shunning mainstream rewards by choice, exert power over one another, over who wears their visual style and who is accepted as having appropriate qualifications. And because social identity must be sustained, the skinhead must continue to earn his qualifications. Visual style is a symbol of group identity for skinheads; it signals 'our way'. For Perth skinheads, being a skinhead means a chance for excitement, a source of identity, and a sense of belonging to something. Being a skinhead is an ethnically-based way of making meaning and sense of the social environment during the liminoid period of adolescence.

Categorical relationships

The visual presentation of the self, or visual style, is used to categorize people in the absence of formal social relationships. Categorization of people through their visual style is also shaped by past experience with persons wearing certain visual styles and by stories told about the experiences of others. Therefore, when entering a crowded pub whose patrons exhibit a variety of clothing and hairstyles, visual style enables skinheads to map the environment, determining friend and potential enemy. Skinheads read visual style and make categorical assumptions about persons wearing particular clothing. Thus anyone wearing mod clothing is usually categorized as a 'wimp'. A person wearing black desert boots, black jeans, black T-shirt, and long hair fits the skinhead conception of a 'bog', and is therefore a potential enemy. This categorical identification applies to some extent to all inhabitants of the city in traffic relationships, but is primarily applied to other youth. A large proportion of youth is placed into the 'straight' category and therefore seen as relatively innocuous.

Certain conclusions about activities in a particular place can also be drawn from clues given by the visual style of its patrons. I was sitting in a pub with Ace, Rhygin and Nutter having an early evening drink. They were discussing where we should go for the evening's entertainment, and listed almost every nightclub in Perth and the reasons for their lack of patronage. They judged the perceived style of each establishment based largely on the visual style of its patrons. For example, they would not go to certain inner-city nightclubs because they are recognized as 'ding' or 'bog' nightclubs due to the perceived large southern European or Australian clienteles. They had also heard reports from others who may have frequented the establishment in the past and commented on the performative style of its patrons. From the establishment's visual style (decor, advertised image) and from the visual style of people entering the establishment, skinheads gauge the type of patron, the sort of music played, the probable response of bouncers to their attempted entry, and the possibility of conflict. In other words, they assess the suitability of various establishments for skinhead entry through clues given by visual and performative style. Some of the reasons given for not entering a particular nightclub were: 'too many dings', 'can't get in there; me and Billy beat up a bouncer', 'can't get in; no skinheads or mods', and 'it's fucked there' or 'they play shit music'. All are evaluative comments on alternative styles and scenes.[7]

Present in these evaluations is the formulating of place through past consociate experience (Sansom 1980, pp.176-91). Skinhead judgement of a particular pub or nightclub often relates to the past experiences of persons and groups in these scenes. One of the quotations listed above, 'can't get in there; me and Billy beat up a bouncer', categorizes the candidate scene as unavailable because of past trouble. To venture again to this scene entails, at best, refusal of entry and, more seriously, the risk of physical danger from the reprisals of bouncers. The availability of inner-city pubs for skinhead daytime drinking also varies. The cycle changes rapidly, usually from week to week, but sometimes from one day to the next. Accordingly, skinhead judgement about possible access 'is designed to accommodate the shifting significance of places in contexts where any given place is liable to mean one thing today and another after the day's action has been completed' (Sansom 1980, p. 177). Some places become permanently off-limits or are regarded with some trepidation. Rhygin never felt very comfortable in one particular nightclub. On an earlier occasion, he had received bruised ribs and an unwanted flight down a steel staircase by courtesy of the bouncers. Therefore, access to any specific place is governed by temporal considerations with respect to past consociate action.

The following event illustrates what may happen if styles are incompatible. En route to a nightclub after drinking in a pub, a set of us passed a flashing neon sign advertising 'Victor's Piano Bar'. Rhygin called, 'Let's go in here for a laugh' and promptly disappeared up a stairwell. The rest, seven of us in all, followed and we found ourselves in a quiet, small, well-furnished bar with a female singing bland love songs accompanied by a male pianist 'tickling the ivories'. The middle-aged couples present talked intimately across their tables. Their facial expressions betrayed their bewilderment as we entered noisily and ordered drinks. The bar attendant made a half-hearted attempt to order us out by asking about the age of the three young women present, but she gave up after being first sworn at and then ignored.

Rhygin, Ace, Nutter and I moved closer to the piano, much to the surprise of the pianist and singer. Ace began trying to 'chat up' the singer in the break between brackets of music. Nutter, Rhygin and I watched his futile attempt while Sue and the other females continued talking amongst themselves. Ace, in his characteristically generous manner, offered the singer a drink from his beer which she politely refused. The singer's discomfort was acutely apparent to Rhygin, Nutter and me, as was that of the other patrons. Ace continued talking with the singer and pianist in his usual amiable manner. Finally, Sue alerted us to the time. We had to leave the bar soon so that we could make it to our nightclub destination before the cover charge for entry rose from A$1 to A$5. As we left via the stairs, one of the skinheads pushed over a large pot plant. He sent it crashing down the stairs, spilling soil and leaves. We emerged onto the street and made our way to the nightclub.

This example highlights the categorical reading of style. Rhygin held certain preconceptions about piano bars and interaction within them. He consciously played upon the perceived difference between the piano bar's style (especially the desired clientele and their behaviour) and that of the skinheads to shock and provide entertainment; to provide a 'good laugh'. The incident also contributed to Rhygin's reputation as a 'mad' and unpredictable character.

The source of subcultural continuity

The contribution of visual style to the social and cultural continuity of the Perth skinhead subculture may be illuminated by contrasting skinheads with another expressive social form, the 'cat' as described by Finestone (1957).[8] The cat is non-violent, violence being reserved for the 'gorillas' of the local scene. Instead, he is 'cool' relying on a repertoire of manipulative techniques to achieve desired ends. He eschews work, choosing the 'hustle' to make his 'bread' – pimping, acting as a con-man, working the illegal numbers racket, or living from the profits of drug supply. The main purpose of his life is the search for the 'kick'. Any activity tabooed by 'squares' (mainstream persons) qualifies as a 'kick', but the most popular kicks usually involve drug experimentation and sexual activity considered perverse by squares. The cat also places great emphasis on sartorial elegance and in creating a new and unusual argot for mundane objects and activities, for example, 'pad' for house, 'pecks' for food, and 'dig the scene' for observing.

The cat is a creature of change. Argot, clothing, the hustle and the kick all express the cat's desired distance and separation from the square world. He is engaged in an effective and extractive relationship with the mainstream world. He lives from the earnings of drug supplying, prostitution, and the illegal numbers racket and scorns the values and lifestyle of the straight world. Most significantly, interaction with the mainstream world, through the custom of his services, is essential for without this exploitative interaction he could not maintain his identity as a cat. Because of interaction between mainstream and ghetto cultures, he must constantly change the social diacritics which mark separation. In order to maintain social and cultural distance, the cat's current argot, musical tastes, and clothing styles must change rapidly as they are appropriated by members of the mainstream.

By contrast, Perth skinheads have no elaborate argot and there is little change in their visual or performative style. Perth skinhead style, the activities in which they engage and the expression of these activities in skinhead uniform, has not changed much in approximately fifteen years. Yet during this period different age grades of young men have entered the subculture, made their mark, and then left the scene. Given these successive waves of recruitment, why does the content of skinhead style remain a remarkably stable expressive form whereas the cat subculture, like youth cultures in general, is characterized by a dynamic of continuous change? The reason for the inertia of visual style lies in the constancy of skinhead opposition to the mainstream world of Australia.

Social and cultural continuity in the skinhead subculture is rooted in this opposition, an opposition which establishes a dichotomy: skinhead versus world. Proof of this position or stance is violence (see Chapter Four). Unlike the cat, skinheads do not have an effective nor an extractive relationship with the world. Skinhead activity occurs in the leisure domain (Hannerz 1980) and is limited to unproductive, non-extractive returns from this activity. They do not depend upon the mainstream world for gain. To become a skinhead is to join a world of exclusivity that can only be mastered and understood through participation in it. Asking a skinhead to tell about violence elicits stories about particular events ('Me and Nutter had a fight with ...') rather than a summary of categories or institutionalized modes of activity. Skinheads do not lack these categories. They refuse to initiate others into their style except through participation. Conceptions of activities such as violence are particularistic not categorical. They deny the transfer of information to unknown outsiders and emphasize the importance of having to be 'one of the lads' to know about skinhead activity. The result is an internal field of skinhead relations and exclusivity that can only be learnt through participation. Proof of this participation is in the narration of stories which highlight personal experience.

The stability of style is structurally rooted in this opposition to the mainstream world. Opposition takes the form of certain modes of activity, chiefly violence, and is expressed in the skinhead uniform. Should the activities comprising performative style change, then the visual style, which signals these activities, would also change;

conversely, changes to visual style would be reflected in changes in performative style. Changes in either performative or visual style thus produce changes in overall style which is a medium for the expression of the skinhead relationship with the mainstream world.

Skinhead visual style is not only shaped by this structural opposition. The uniform must also be inexpensive. Few teenagers can afford to spend more than several hundred dollars. Buying the skinhead uniform is cheap when compared with, for example, buying a motorbike, an essential feature for claiming 'bikie' identity. A person may buy all the necessary basic skinhead gear for an initial outlay of less than A$400. (Costs at the time of research: Doc Marten boots = A$90, haircut = A$5, jeans = A$45, denim or flight-jacket = A$45, and several T-shirts). Compare this cost to the outlay of a surfer (surfboard, wetsuits, transport for surfboard) or a bikie (anywhere up to $15,000 depending on the type and size of the motorbike).

Although tangential to my discussion of subcultural continuity, a brief departure is required to explain the absence of any elaborate skinhead argot. Accounts of subcultures are marked by the exclusion of outsiders through the knowledge of, and linguistic competence in, a group-specific argot. Why then does a self-conscious, self-identified subculture such as that of the skinheads have such a poorly developed argot? One clue can be found in another exception to this general rule, the beat scene studied by Polsky (1971). He found that 'the individuals in question [beats] resent any label whatever, and regard a concern with labelling as basically square' (Polsky 1971, p. 149). Like skinheads, beats do not depend upon the world for gain; beats grow their beards and collectively turn their backs on the square world just as skinheads mark their opposition to the mainstream world by the aggressive uniform. Unlike the cat, there is little need to mark one's distance from the mainstream through a constantly-evolving argot. Skinhead argot is also sparse because subcultural items are limited. While many hours could be spent discussing the relative merits of a Harley Davidson motorbike over a Japanese copy, discussion about Doc Marten boots would soon be exhausted. Emphasis is placed on action rather than expression, so elaborate argot is replaced by stories about this action.

Another reason for the sparse skinhead argot is that, in keeping with the skinhead focus on physical action, emphasis in storytelling calls for the development of mimetic rather than verbal skills. Ace tells a good story because his speaking is accompanied by the physical re-enactment of the event. A story about a fight is informed not with a profusion of apposite descriptive words, but by demonstrative gestures – the punching of the air, a mimed head-butt, a clenched fist. The 'down-to-earth' ethos of the skinhead (Hebdige 1982, p. 29) means that he is not concerned with artistic production. To the skinhead, such artistic orientation is that of a poseur and is evidenced in Perth in the lifestyle of the contemptible mod.

Related to this denial of life as art is the particularistic, rather than categorical, description of social life. Participation and authenticity are not divorced in social life. Being a skinhead involves doing skinhead things. Little time is spent reflecting on a philosophy of life, only on one's performance in life's action. The aesthetic cool of the cat has no place in skinhead social life where the measure of a man is his record of subcultural performance, regardless of his verbal agility. Discussion of events is place and person-specific. No social type emerges except in the most general of terms: the hard, loyal skinhead. What is left is no self-conscious articulation of what being a skinhead is (with the accompanying argot for description of the hustle and kick). Rather, a picture emerges by piecing together stories about consociate experience. While the cat is a creature of fantasy, of the creation of himself as a successful hustler living from his ill-gotten gains and pursuing his kicks, the pragmatic skinhead, while also striving to create his own reputation as 'hard', must have proof of his subcultural performances. The cat is a con-man, a hustler and a boaster. The skinhead is, to borrow Rhygin's phrase, 'a man of action not words'. In the next chapter I begin to examine some of this action.

Notes

1. For an appreciation of the myriad eccentricities and detail in clothing styles one should refer to Ferguson's (1982) original article. The main point here is to establish the variety of styles worn and their approximate order chronologically. For a discussion of more recent clothing styles, see Marshall (1991).

2. For the young women who associate with Perth skinheads, the hair cut described by Ferguson is sometimes seen (i.e., a 'feather cut' – a skinhead crop with a long fringe), but more often a longer variation.

3. My comments about the pattern evident in the accounts of being labelled 'Poms' on arrival in Perth (Chapter One) are pertinent here.

4. See Marsh, Rosser and Hame (1978) for a discussion of generational levels amongst English football supporters.

5. Madness, an English music band which toured Australia in the early 1980s, was popular with members of the English scene.

6. In the future, it would be interesting to note the possible repercussions of the appropriation of items of skinhead uniform by non-skinhead youth. In Perth, Doc Marten boots used to be 'skinhead boots' worn only by members of that style. At present, Doc Martens boots, both black and oxblood, are being worn more and more by youth defined by skinheads as 'trendies'. How much of English visual style is filtering to non-English youth? Will skinhead visual style change as a result of increasing appropriation or will skinheads continue to defend the integrity of their style?

7. Denial of entry is rare for mods and they are usually welcome in most nightclubs unless mistaken for skinheads, as some undifferentiating Australian doormen tend to do. On the other hand, preventing skinheads and mods from entering could be designed to catch out skinheads dressed as mods, but it seems unduly harsh on the genuine mods.

8. Finestone conducted intensive interviews between 1951 and 1953 in Chicago with over fifty male, African American heroin users in their late teens and early twenties. The interviewees were selected from 'several of the areas of highest incidence of drug use' and his interviews were designed to elicit common attitudes, values, modes of behaviour, and social orientation.

4 Ritual violence and symbolic solidarity

Labels such as 'mindless', 'sick', and 'senseless' are often used to describe interpersonal violence amongst youth, the traditional folk devils. However, such vivid descriptions obscure the underlying motives and meanings of these actions for the actors involved.[1] Social rules govern violence and these rules render violence intelligible and rewarding for those who participate in it.

The stance of the skinhead

Skinheads evince an aggressive stance towards the world. Skinhead violence, or 'aggro', is the proof which authenticates this claimed position. As I noted in Chapter Three, Perth skinheads hold little idea of how English skinheads behave. Instead, in the migrant experience, certain stereotypes about English skinhead behaviour are transported to Australia, most notably clothing style and conceptions of English skinheads as violent. Of these two surviving impressions, the perceived link between skinheads and 'aggro' is paramount and is demonstrated in numerous conversations devoted to the subject, as the following example suggests. One Friday night, Rhygin, Ace, Terry, Jack, Roy, Nutter, Karen and I were sitting drinking beer in the lounge of Terry's flat. After a discussion of varied topics, the conversation turned to fighting and the notion of 'hardness'. A debate began about what being 'hard' consisted of; what did a skinhead have to do to be collectively judged as 'hard' by other skinheads? Rhygin thought hardness meant 'never backing down, no matter what the odds are', even if physical injury was imminent. Hypothetical situations were invented: 'What would you do if twenty boongs came down the street carrying steel pipes and wooden pickets?' For Rhygin, being hard meant the skinhead would stay and fight the Aborigines. Winning fights was important in Rhygin's definition but, essentially, being hard meant being brave or fearless. Other skinheads, particularly Jack, disagreed with Rhygin. Collectively, they thought a hard skinhead to be 'someone who wins his fights'. Rhygin's 'hard skin' was redefined as a 'nutter' by the other skinheads present.[2] Despite differences between the two definitions, both involve fighting and the skinhead's preparedness to fight. The debate became heated at times and revealed the importance of hardness for these skinheads.

But violence is not only a personal expression of skinhead stance. More importantly, violence collectively affirms categorical skinhead identity through displays of group solidarity. Skinheads take decisive action against persons they interpret as symbolically or actually threatening this solidarity. By fighting side-by-side, skinheads symbolically signal their common categorical identity in the test of actual combat. Sometimes a skinhead does not measure up in this crucial physical test, choosing to leave a potentially dangerous situation. His action will usually bring scorn from other skinheads, especially if the deserted skinheads are also close consociates. 'Standing with yer mates' formed the basis for much skinhead talk. Again, in conversation, hypothetical test situations were proposed and pledges of allegiance elicited to reinforce solidarity. Solidarity is central to being a skinhead and is expressed in stance and the symbolic act of violence. The cry, 'The lads in action!' which I heard one night shortly after a fight, describes a symbolic act which reasserts skinhead solidarity.

A skinhead cannot claim to be a 'skin' if he does not fight. Everything about the skinhead uniform unequivocally signals one's preparedness for violence and one does not don the uniform without accepting the implications. As soon as he crosses his doorstep and moves into the public urban scene, the skinhead has issued his challenge. He must assume that he will attract hostility by his wearing of skinhead uniform and to remain a skinhead means accepting the consequences of this challenge. Some grow tired of relating to the world in this way and leave the subculture. In the words of one ex-skinhead, who had exchanged his crop and boots for the relative safety of teddy boy style, 'I was sick of always having to look over my shoulder when I went out'.

Violence generally occurs in the public domain. Part of the experience of most skinheads involves interaction with police and also with civil custodians such as hotel and nightclub bouncers. The police represent a generalized threat, one that must constantly be taken into account in the public scene. Most skinheads can tell stories about perceived victimization, being singled out 'because I'm a skinhead'. I heard about one such incident, concerning two skinheads en route to the airport, from one of the skinheads involved. He told a group of us about his experience. The storyteller was a passenger in a car and had been resting his arm on the sill of the car's open window. The vehicle was stopped by a traffic policeman who served an infringement notice for 'having my arm out the window'. The practice of resting one's arm on the window-sill, while illegal, is by no means uncommon during Perth's hot summers but this skinhead felt his style had been responsible for undue zeal on the part of the policeman.

Skinheads are hardly unaware of their visual impact in the city. Their clothing is loud and aggressive, but this is desirable as loudness of visual style sets the skinhead apart from all others. Aggressive presentation of the self establishes the basis for categorical relationships within the public scene. For the police, skinhead visual style signals trouble and few members of the public are unfamiliar with popular myths about skinheads generated by the media. In the public mind, violence and skinheads are inextricably linked and a stereotypic vision shapes the categorical relationships between the skinheads and the public. For the on-scene civil guardians, hotel and nightclub bouncers, this categorical identification can be modified by extensive knowledge of specific identities. In a regular venue, bouncers are familiar with skinhead regulars whereas in the intermittent, shared venue, the categorical view of skinheads as violent and potentially disruptive prevails. Hence three skinheads were once refused entry into a fashionable nightclub on the grounds that 'no short hair' was allowed. On another occasion I witnessed, several skinheads were reluctantly admitted to a nightclub with the warning, 'We don't want any trouble in here, boys. You know what happens to skinheads who cause trouble here'.

Skinhead violence

There are three recurring themes in skinhead violence:

1   The public opportunity to demonstrate loyalty to:
    i.   skinheads as a whole if the threat is from outside the skinhead subculture or
    ii. to one's closest friends if the threat is from inside the skinhead subculture.
2   A chance to further one's reputation as a skinhead.

3   Fighting is an essential part of the 'good nights' ethic.

Three categories of skinhead violence can be distinguished with reference to the identities of protagonists:

1   Skinhead versus skinhead conflict.
2   Skinhead versus English scene member, that is, mod, teddy boy, rockabilly, or punk.
3   Skinhead versus outsiders, that is, those from outside the English scene – usually bogs, a generic term which includes Aborigines and those of Italian, Greek or Anglo-Celtic origins, or other persons involved in the urban nightlife who are not part of the English scene.

The concept of 'ritual' is apposite to describe behaviour in the three categories of violence involving skinheads. Ritual, as it is used here, describes the different routines and symbolic actions that are followed in violent situations and performed before an audience, even if the audience is other skinheads also participating in the ritual. Skinheads perform rituals of violence when their solidarity is threatened by outsiders. Symbolically, violence provides the chance to show worthiness as a skinhead, by 'standing with yer mates', and reaffirms collective solidarity.

The ritual of violence differs for each category of violence because the symbolic threat encountered differs for each category. There is a qualitative difference between violence of Categories 1 and 2 and violence of Category 3 because the subcultural members of Categories 1 and 2 are all part of the English scene. The resolution of conflict depends largely on the networks of those involved. If there exists a weak tie between the opposing forces, forged in a past consociate era, then the chances of resolution are enhanced. For instances of violence involving members of the English scene, a peaceful resolution is more likely because there is a greater chance of a network link between opposed sets. The ritual which serves to control skinhead versus skinhead violence also applies, to some extent, to conflict with members of other groups who move between the same set of scenes, that is, English scene members. The ritual is completely different for Category 3, skinhead versus outsider, because there is no history of common participation in scenes and eras. There is little chance of a weak link existing between the warring parties. As I detailed in Chapter Three, some skinheads do establish links with bogs through common participation in what I termed 'day style' but this is by no means common. If there are no links between the two opposing forces, categorical relationships inform behaviour. Perhaps the best way to demonstrate these differences is to present ethnographic material to illustrate each category of conflict.

Skinhead versus skinhead conflict

A ritual of restraint operates when skinhead fights skinhead. Altercations between skinheads rarely reach the physical stage. If they do, action is swiftly taken by others to ensure a speedy resolution, hopefully satisfactory to those involved. Rather than risk conflict within the category (and especially within the quasi-group), and thus present a weaker front to the outside world, skinheads aim to solve internal altercations before violence occurs and threatens their precarious social unity. The desire for resolution is not so evident when the protagonists are of little note in the skinhead scheme.

Pamela is the girlfriend of Den, a well-known skinhead. She was 'after' (had stated her intention to assault) two punk females, Tiffany and Debbie. Rhygin's girlfriend at the time, Jane, who is a close friend of the two punks, heard about Pamela's threat and confronted her one afternoon in a city pub. (Interestingly, Jane is placing her friendship with the two punks above the identity she shares with Pamela – as young women who associate with skinheads.[3]) There was a heated verbal exchange which ended when Jane left the pub with Rhygin to meet Tiffany and Debbie outside. The four of them then began walking away from the pub. After walking for a few moments, a shout of 'Jane!' was heard from across the street where Pamela was walking with another young woman, Anne. Pamela's 'boyfriend', Den, and Anne's partner, Nick, were walking about twenty yards ahead on the same side of the street. While Tiffany and Debbie left the scene hurriedly, Jane immediately stepped across the road and began arguing with Pamela. Rhygin followed but kept his distance. Once the verbal exchange between the two young women became physical he moved to intercede but was grabbed and kicked in the face by Den, who said, 'What do you think you're doing?' Rhygin backed away from the two males. Jane was still embroiled with Pamela but was holding her own despite Pamela's superior physical strength. She then managed to extricate herself from the entanglement and joined Rhygin some ten yards away. After more heated words the two parties went their separate ways.

The incident worries Rhygin because he knows that Den and Nick both visit Darcy's regularly (also Rhygin's regular leisure venue) and might decide to continue the disagreement. Another consideration is Nick's friendship with the legendary skinhead Robbo thus risking Robbo's involvement in the argument on Nick's side. Amongst Rhygin's consociates loyalty is declared: Rhygin will not be alone if there is any trouble. Despite these pledges there is a feeling, voiced by some, that it is not good having to decide between parties in an argument between skinheads. Rhygin feels apprehensive the next Friday evening when we arrive at Darcy's. Many of his friends are there but Rhygin does not relish having to 'watch his back' as well as being the potential cause of a sizeable conflict between skinheads. On his return from a visit to the toilet, Rhygin tells me that Den had stepped into his path. Instead of the expected trouble, Den had offered his handshake to end the 'misunderstanding'.

The argument between Rhygin and Den did not originate from an outside threat to skinhead solidarity. Rather, a fight between two females, Pamela and Jane, could have been the cause of a division within skinhead ranks. The choice for Den lay between continuing the disagreement with Rhygin over the actions of their respective partners and thereby risking skinhead unity, or settling the matter peacefully and to the satisfaction of both parties. Choosing the former option would yield little reward. Both Den and Rhygin would be blamed for causing the split by those who had voiced their discomfort over choosing sides. Den, in the interests of this unity, chose the latter option.

This particular incident also raises questions about gender relations. The interests of skinhead solidarity took precedence over the disagreement between Den and Rhygin. Skinheads would say that the original argument was unimportant because it was between two females, Jane and Pamela, but I think that such a judgement requires qualification. Much would depend on the relationship between the skinhead and his female partner. Should a skinhead have a serious and regular partner (which is relatively rare) then this relationship may take precedence in an altercation. However, rarely would two skinheads cause conflict and a disruption of skinhead solidarity over an argument between two young women. If one or both did so, they would be allocating higher value to their non-skinhead relationships. In most cases, skinhead solidarity would assume priority and relegate the relationship between a skinhead and his partner to a secondary position. Much would also depend on the identity of the two fighting skinheads. If they do not know each other well or actively dislike each other, the argument between females might be used as an excuse for conflict. However, I never witnessed nor heard of any incidents of this type.

Skinhead versus English scene member

In conflict between skinheads and other members of the English scene, bloodless resolution often depends on the networks of the opposing persons or groups. Should there be a link between the two groups, the ritual will resemble that when two skinheads 'sort things out'. Those persons who know one another take the initiative to begin peace proceedings. On other occasions no such links exist and in their absence fierce fighting may take place. The controlling ritual is abandoned for another, that of a 'kicking', if the opponent is alone, or a 'scrap', if there are numbers on both sides. Sometimes, even though a link may exist, one or both protagonists may refuse to enter into negotiations thus leaving the lads who are friends from some past era in an awkward position. They will then either opt out of the potential trouble or once it has started act to minimize the physical combat. The latter option is more often exercised as this prevents accusations of cowardice which may be levelled at the friends if they take no action in the dispute. In the following example the existing friendships between individual members of the opposed sets were not strong enough to prevent trouble.

Several skinheads had decided to begin their evening at a suburban pub. Present on this particular occasion were many older ex-skins as well as a substantial mod faction. One of the skinheads, Pete, spied a mod with whom he'd had a long-standing argument. It dated from some earlier trouble when the mod had beaten up one of Pete's friends, Scouse. Pete declared his intent to 'have' the mod during the evening and gained verbal support from the other skinheads present. While Pete moved around the venue trying to elicit further support, a mod named Danny, who knew Rhygin, came over to talk with him. Danny also brought along the mod who was the planned target and introduced him to Rhygin. The two mods then left. Rhygin speculated as to whether Danny, realizing that Pete was plotting an assault, had tried to establish some link, however flimsy, between Rhygin and the targeted mod. Rhygin's tie with Danny was not very close. They had been acquainted when Danny was a skinhead, a year or so before, but had never been close friends. Later, trouble did start despite Rhygin's attempts at prevention. It seems that Pete felt strongly enough about the past incident to ignore both Rhygin's protests and the tie between Rhygin and Danny. He risked trouble within the English scene to reassert, symbolically, skinhead solidarity with Scouse.

In this situation the relationship between Rhygin and Danny was not strong enough to prevent conflict. This is not to suggest that Pete would have necessarily chosen the conciliatory option, merely that the option did not exist in any real sense. The ritual began with the declaring of intent, followed by the non-verbal communicative signs (eyeing-up), and the collecting of oaths from allies ('I'm in') to build a strong front against the opponent's forces. It was then carried through to its logical, violent conclusion. However, only a few weeks after the incident, Danny appeared at Darcy's and resolved the dispute with Pete.[4]

Why did Pete choose not to assault Danny when they met at Darcy's? Certainly, the other skinheads present asked this question and considered Pete a 'dickhead' for not taking revenge. Central to this incident is the interplay between the group opinion and that of Pete. The group's role is to announce the skinhead ethos and suggest that Danny be punished for his part in the episode. Pete's role involves the personalization of the feud. Considering his planned visit to England only months later, to take action against Danny could jeopardize the trip. If the police became involved there may have been legal proceedings preventing him from leaving Australia. In this way, situational and temporal factors may become significant. When Pete was required to plan for his future and consider the potential legal ramifications of present decisions, he chose to ignore the subcultural pressure to assault Danny and to accept a possible loss of status. His refusal to fight Danny also rests partly on his own generally easy-going disposition, choosing to forget the incident rather than risk further trouble. In addition, he would prefer to be able to visit Darcy's without having to watch Danny for further trouble. It was also undeniably in Danny's best interests for similar reasons. Danny and Pete both move in the English scene and their paths would inevitably cross again in the future.

The incident and its aftermath demonstrate the struggle between group ideology and personality style and illustrates the supremacy of the latter in Perth skinhead social relationships. Because Pete is an established personality within the subculture his decision to forgive and forget is accepted, albeit grudgingly. Had he been someone of lesser note in the skinhead world, the decision would perhaps have been made for him by the others. Was his reputation tarnished by his backing down? I think not. Taking into account situational exigencies – the planned trip and Danny's involvement in the same scene –

together with Pete's proven history of willingness to fight, his reputation emerged relatively unscathed. However, the incident is rarely discussed. It was a situation in which there was neither a clear winner nor an obvious loser and from which little satisfaction could be gained.

However, conflict between skinheads and other members of the English scene is not always resolved so readily. Rhygin and I had arranged to meet Ace at Johnno's Bar. Darcy's, the regular venue, had become boring. Johnno's is a 1950s bar which played rock 'n' roll music and we had heard good reports from those who had spent time there. We arrived and met Ace, Roy, Pete, Di, Michelle, Karen, Sandie, and Tim. For the first part of the evening the young women danced while the lads stood at the bar 'having a laugh' and a drink or two. Shortly before 11 p.m. I noticed Rhygin glaring in the direction of a group of rockabillies, male and female, whose numbers had been small earlier in the evening but had built up as the night progressed. He then turned and spoke quietly to Ace. I asked Rhygin what was going on and he replied, 'John's here'. John was a rockabilly who had 'gone out with' Sarah, one of Rhygin's past girlfriends, immediately after Rhygin and Sarah had split up. Rhygin declared he was going to 'get that bastard tonight!' Events began to develop around Rhygin's declared intention to assault John. Ace voiced his physical support for Rhygin should John get the better of him. Rhygin replied that Ace was not to intervene if he was gaining the upper hand. However, if John appeared to be the victor, Ace was only to end the fight before Rhygin was injured. Ace retorted that if John was winning he would 'kick his head in'. Roy indicated his willingness to fight. So did Pete, who'd left the pub briefly and had returned after a failed attempt to 'get off with a bird'. Appraised of the situation, Pete announced in his customary impassive manner, 'I'm in if it starts'. For the next half an hour Rhygin steeled himself for the clash while John remained unaware of the mounting threat.

Matt, an ex-skinhead who used to associate with Rhygin but was now a rockabilly, arrived at Johnno's around 11.30 p.m. He was told of Rhygin's intentions. Being a friend of John's, Matt began to try and dissuade Rhygin from causing trouble. He said that if they did 'start' (fighting) he would not take sides but would try to separate them. He asked Rhygin 'to forget the whole thing', which Rhygin refused to do. Rhygin became somewhat confused. He wanted to confront John but had to consider the part Matt might play in the impending drama and had also to consider intervention by the pub bouncers. Finally, Rhygin walked over to John and '[head]butted' him lightly on the forehead, more a warning and provocation than an attack. Matt interceded before any of the other skinheads or rockabillies could act, and led Rhygin to a table where they talked for about ten minutes. Then Matt left Rhygin to talk with the rockabillies. Over the next twenty minutes the two opposing groups kept their distance, the skinheads waiting to choose the moment to strike while the rockabillies banded around John to show their loyalty to him.

About midnight, John and the other rockabillies left the pub with the skinheads following them around to the side of the building. John was able to slip into the bar again (through a side door) after explaining his predicament to one of the bouncers. John, the focus of Rhygin's anger, was now out of reach and it seemed the situation would defuse. Suddenly, Roy stepped forward and butted Tex, a rockabilly, splitting the skin over his eyebrow and causing a wound that began to bleed profusely. This brought an immediate and angry response from the rockabillies and also from one skinhead, Johnny, who knew many of the rockabillies and had spent most of his evening talking to them. Johnny's forceful response to Roy's act was, 'What the fuck did you do that for?' He moved towards Roy threateningly. At this point Ace, who knew Johnny fairly well, stepped between them and tried to cool Johnny down. Roy looked on, neither repentant nor scared. Johnny's friendship with the rockabillies complicated the categorical skinhead versus rockabilly conflict. The collective mood of the rockabillies (and of the staff of Johnno's, some of whom had ventured outside to watch the confrontation) changed with Roy's unprovoked assault and many verbal threats were issued. One of the staff yelled, 'Get going before I call the cops'. We moved away slowly with one bouncer calling to Roy, 'I'll remember you, I'll get you!'[5] Roy's response was a defiant 'Fuck off!'

About ten minutes passed. Roy had left the scene and those of us who remained decided to go to a nightclub. This meant walking back past the rockabillies. We passed them without physical incident although the tension was palpable and the verbal abuse bitter. We were about thirty yards past when Rhygin picked up a piece of rock and hurled it back into the rockabillies/staff group. This brought more angry cries but we did not wait to discover their response. Ace yelled, 'Run!' and the three of us tore up an alleyway behind the pub and into a large car park. It was only then that we realized the others had not made the same decision. After a few moments hiding in some bushes, the coast seemed clear. We ventured back down the alleyway to be met by the others who were clearly upset by our hasty exit. It transpired that the rockabillies had attacked Pete. The young women, in coming to his aid, had been assaulted too.

The young women were clearly furious claiming, 'we got beaten up for you'. The main target of their anger was Rhygin as it was he who had thrown the rock and then deserted them, or so they thought. Pete said nothing as he understood the logic of our flight – that we were outnumbered and it was therefore better to run. The reasoning was that the females would be safe because the opponents would not assault them if they were by themselves. However, for Pete the complication was that one of the young women, Sandie, was his sister. He felt he could not run off and leave her despite the 'women alone' reasoning. He had stayed and received numerous cuts to his ear and face.

In the eyes of the females, Rhygin was responsible for the new round of trouble, yet he had deserted them in the face of superior numbers. Rhygin threw the rock after tempers had been soothed. The situation had been resolved or, more accurately, had petered out with Ace's placating of Johnny after Roy's assault on Tex. Tim, Pete, and the females were attacked by the incensed rockabillies and, with the exception of Pete, vented their anger on Rhygin. First, they felt Rhygin had caused the new round of trouble and, second, after causing it had left them to deal with the consequences of his actions. On his return, Rhygin was challenged on the issue of solidarity by Tim and the females. He had performed a symbolic faux pas. Had Rhygin thrown the rock and then stayed, the reaction from the others would have been different. However, because Rhygin had deserted the 'birds' and Tim (who was not a skinhead nor even an acquaintance of Rhygin's) the incident had little effect on Rhygin's reputation amongst other skinheads. As I said, Pete understood Rhygin's reasons for fleeing and perhaps other skinheads did too. (I never found out because the incident was not discussed.) Rhygin also has an impressive record of past performances in more serious situations involving the expression of solidarity with other skinheads.

Another example of behaviour in this category of violent situation also has Rhygin as its central character. In Chapter Three I described the exchange between Rhygin and the young man wearing an Oi! T-shirt which ended in a scuffle (page 55). Here I want to deal with the violent aspects of this incident. At the conclusion of the verbal exchange, Rhygin had leapt to his feet, strode to where the T-shirt wearer was standing and 'nutted' (head-butted) him. I turned to Dennis and Chris, who had also seen what was happening but had made no move to go to Rhygin's aid. I suggested, 'I think we should go and stop it, or help him'. Chris replied tentatively, 'Let's go and have a look'. I hurried over and stepped between Rhygin and a second opponent in an effort to calm things down. The second youth that I was restraining stated menacingly, 'You better get your mate away or he's in big trouble'. He recognized my role as the ritual mediator in the drama. We moved back to our table and then left the pub, noticing the congregation of bouncers who had gathered to see what the commotion was about. There were no consociate ties between the two sets but the presence of superior numbers on one side, the proximity of the hotel bouncers, and my mediation were enough to ensure a relatively minor incident.

In the postmortem of the incident, Rhygin accused Dennis and Chris of not helping him out when he needed his mates. They countered by saying that they were there if needed. Rhygin thought this unsatisfactory and cited the example of an earlier session at the same pub when he had involved in a fight in the car park. Ace came over to the car and 'hit the first person he didn't know'. This, thought Rhygin, was the correct way of helping a mate in trouble. In his eyes, Dennis and Chris had failed to express their solidarity with him in the symbolic act of violence. Later discussions of the incident with other skinheads elicited similar responses. Both Terry and Ace thought Dennis and Chris 'wimps' for not aiding Rhygin. Had they been in the pub, they said they would have gone over to the table with Rhygin rather than waiting to see what developed. My behaviour was seen as acceptable for I had moved quickly to help Rhygin and had therefore put myself at risk on his behalf. I was also excused somewhat as I was not a skinhead and was therefore not wholly bound by the same code of 'standing with yer mates'.

Skinhead versus outsider

One Thursday evening, Rhygin, Terry, Nutter, Rachel, Ace, and I were at Darcy's. Around 11.45 p.m., a scuffle broke out on the far side of the pub. Apparently a skinhead named Cally, who was known to the set I was with, had an argument with another patron. Cally invited him outside to continue the disagreement and when he refused to go Cally assaulted him inside the pub. The fight was broken up by bouncers who escorted the protagonists to the door. On his way to the door, Cally's opponent protested at his removal. For his trouble he was dealt several vicious blows by one of the bouncers who then dumped him on the pavement in front of the pub. Within seconds Cally, and three other skinheads I did not know at the time, descended upon the dazed man and proceeded to 'kick him in', raining kicks upon his head and torso. The assault ended abruptly with another skinhead reminding the attackers of the possible arrival of the police and those involved hurriedly left the scene. Considering the ferocity of the attacks (both from the bouncer and the skinheads) the victim, after being revived, looked in fair condition apart from a bloody nose and already-darkening bruises. An image that remains with me is of Roy chanting, 'Cal-ley, Cal-ley' with his fist upheld and clenched, reminiscent of a British football chant. The fist was symbolic of the night's achievement and expressive of the pride engendered by the incident.

The ritual aspects of the incident centre on Cally and his relationship with his fellow attackers. The victim had threatened Cally in what the skinheads regarded as their venue. This threat was, in turn, perceived as a threat to all those skinheads who were present and who knew Cally. Cally's friends seized the opportunity to prove their worth in the skinhead scheme through their violent support of him. The threat was symbolic as the opponent posed no real threat to them all physically but had insulted their categorical skinhead identity. There is usually no such thing as an attack on a single skinhead. If a skinhead is accompanied, then the threat to him is also perceived as a threat to the action-set and they too will act. In this case the threat was external. There was no need for mediation because the potential victim was unknown. The repercussions, apart from trouble with the police, would not pose problems of divisions within skinhead networks or the English scene. It was the expression of a self-fulfilling prophecy I heard repeated in several contexts, but always applied to violence with persons or groups outside the English scene, 'When we get one of them alone we do it to them 'cos if it was one of us alone they'd do it to us'.

The applicability of this maxim was demonstrated by another incident which also occurred one evening at Darcy's. Most members of the group with whom I moved were there, as were many other skinheads and members of the English scene. About halfway through the evening, Rhygin appeared through the noisy crowd and told me of an encounter that had taken place only moments before in the toilet. He, Jack and Ace had been involved in an argument with a drunken man. This man, who also had a beard and shoulder-length hair, had asked the skinheads if having long hair meant 'you were slow or something'. Rhygin had replied, 'Well you must be a fucking retard then!' (Later I found out that the argument was over needing to have short hair to be accepted by skinheads.) The trio had then left the toilet laughing.

Later in the pub proper I saw the same man confronting Jack at the bar. Rhygin was standing to Jack's right. I moved over and stood near Rhygin realizing that trouble was brewing. I was also attempting to listen to another conversation between Ace and Smithy when Rhygin grabbed my arm, pulled me into his conversation and said belligerently to the bearded man, 'Look, he's got long hair but he's all right with us!' (While my hair was long by comparison with the skinhead crop it was still short in relation to the bearded man's.) Jack was staring intently at the man, who continued arguing with Rhygin and then turned to walk away. Jack said, 'Fuck off then, you bastard!' By now Roy and some of the other skinheads had noticed the altercation and were moving towards Jack. As the bearded man passed Roy, Roy pushed and cursed him. Now one of the bouncers arrived. He spoke first to the bearded man (who was now with two friends – one male, one female) and then to Jack and Roy. After the bouncer had left, discussion focused on assaulting the bearded man outside, away from the attentions of the bouncers. After another verbal exchange between the bearded man and the skinheads and further intervention by the bouncer, the bearded man's friends persuaded him to leave. Roy, Nutter, Jack and several others followed. Rhygin and I remained inside the pub.

When the others returned their accounts were confused. It seemed that they had 'put the boot in' to the bearded man. One had grabbed his hair and started butting him in the face while others were kicking him. Apparently some of his mates had turned up but would not fight. The accounts of this event show the emphasis placed on hardness by skinheads. Several stated, with begrudging admiration, that the bearded man, despite 'getting hammered', managed to stay on his feet throughout the assault and to continue haranguing them. They said, 'He wouldn't go down'.

Part of being a skinhead is showing your support for other skinheads. The bearded man provided the opportunity to display this support by threatening Jack in the skinheads' regular venue. As in the Cally example, this was interpreted by the others as a symbolic threat to them all. The verbal exchange was present, followed by the demonstrated loyalty of other skinheads to Jack, and finally the denouement in the alleyway.

The significance of aggro

Present in the three types of conflict presented above are the three themes noted at the beginning of the chapter. Demonstrating loyalty, furthering your own reputation, and completing a part of the 'good nights' ethic, all combine to make skinhead fighting very much a group affair. Public acts of violence also guarantee an audience to record one's performances. Fighting is the physical proof of a fundamental skinhead value – 'to stand with yer mates'. Proving loyalty to mates symbolically reaffirms the collective, categorical nature of skinhead unity. Suggestive of the importance of aggro are the many conversations on the subject – discussions of past fights, the actions of those involved, and the cognitive ranking of hardness. The incidence of actual violence, the projection of this violent group identity to the mainstream world, and the roles particular persons play in these aims are focal concerns for the skinhead subculture. An important conclusion which may be drawn from the three themes is their contribution to performative and consociate identity. Recalling my comments on stance, a skinhead's identity derives primarily from his performance in fighting. One cannot claim skinhead identity unless one fights. This leads to a consideration of skinhead reputation.

Acts of violence have important consequences for a skinhead's ranking in the eyes of other skinheads. The investment of one's time, energy, and the risk of physical injury to prove loyalty, is repaid in the form of conceded reputation. The number of 'good times' credited to a skinhead can be equated with his social worth, and thus his position within the subculture. The immediate past is mapped through these good times and scenes also assigned degrees of safety or risk on the basis of past events associated with them. In a subculture where you are what you do, or have done, you have a stake in constructing the past via such events. Once you have accumulated enough good times and satisfactory performances to your credit, you have earned the right to wear the style, to be recognized as 'one of the lads'. Exceptional performance in fights earns one the title of 'hard' and the respect it entails.

My use of the term 'ritual' to describe and understand violent incidents is similar to that of Colburn (1985) in his study of violence among professional ice hockey players in Canada. There is one major difference between the rituals of violence he describes and the rituals informing skinhead fighting – the notion of a 'fair fight'. In the world of ice hockey, the fair fight is underscored by a commonly-held players' conception of personal honour. Thus the fist-fights which Colburn describes are a result of, and attempt to deter, 'cheap-shots' (illegal assaults as defined by the players' own informal code) which show little respect for the victim of the cheap-shot, for the formal rules, or for the unwritten players' code of ice hockey. Moreover, their notion of honour as solely personal means that one person's honour is not transferable to another. A player is expected to act as the guardian of his own honour and to avoid disputes involving the honour of others.

Skinheads differ from ice hockey professionals in two related ways. Skinheads do not have a concept of honour. Instead, they have their categorical skinhead identity which may be undermined if a skinhead fails to respond to a perceived threat. Second, while this categorical identity is, to some degree, vested in the individual, it is glossed over by the primacy accorded to a group conception of solidarity.[6] Skinhead acts of violence reaffirm not the rules of a formalized game but skinhead solidarity towards non-skinhead others. Any possibility of a fair fight is denied by the belief noted earlier, 'When we get one of them alone we do it to them 'cos if it was one of us alone they'd do it to us'. To fight fairly yields no rewards for skinhead solidarity nor for personal reputation. As the skinheads arguing with Rhygin over the definition of 'hard' put the matter, a hard skinhead is one who wins his fights. No consolation is awarded to the skinhead who fights fairly but loses his fights. Skinhead fighting, then, is primarily a symbolic expression of solidarity rather than a personal mode of action in the face of threat.

A further difference between ice hockey professionals and Perth skinheads is that most skinhead violence occurs between skinheads and non-skinheads, that is, between persons not of the same category.[7] Fighting is severely limited when the protagonists are both skinheads, that is, drawn from the same category. Usually, it is only when protagonists are drawn from outside the category that serious fighting occurs. When fighting others from the English scene, links of association must be taken into account before a decision is made. Violent interaction with people completely outside the English scene is more often serious. Both sides know that there are no holds barred. It is relevant to mention here that the most talked about fights are those with outsiders. This fact stems from a reluctance to highlight internal divisions, but also from the reality that more happens in a skinhead versus outsider clash because the ritual informing behaviour is, as I have shown, less restricting.

Ritual violence is the ultimate symbolic expression of group loyalty and symbolic solidarity, one so central to the skinhead world view that without it one could not claim true skinhead identity, or be granted that status by others. I close this chapter with a comment made by Rhygin, after a fight in which a skinhead from one group had been aided by several from another group despite the fact that he had not met them before:

> If there hadn't been a fight we would have still been friends but, as Scouse and Ace said, because they picked on Smithy and we jumped in and helped, it formed a bond. We arranged to go back the following Saturday.

Some interaction between skinheads and other members of the English scene is not so violent. In the next chapter I examine what happens when skinheads interact with members of other youth subcultures in a more sociable manner.

Notes

1. The literature on violence is limited mostly to psychological explanations of the motives for aggression by 'unstable individuals'. Most studies also deal with violence of a serious nature, that is, murder, rape and armed robbery (e.g., Toch 1969), without considering the social implications of violent acts. An alternative to the psychological view is the ethological perspective which views violence as an innate drive (e.g., Fox 1976, Lorenz 1970, Tiger 1972). More useful approaches, anthropological or sociological, can be found in Bienen (1968), Colburn (1985), Dyck (1980), Hepburn (1973), Marsh (1978), Marsh, Rosser and Hame (1978), Marx (1976), and Walter (1969). In the latter studies, authors address the social factors operating in any violent situation and the social rewards gained from violence within certain social settings.

2. 'Hard' parallels the notion of 'rep' (reputation) and 'heart' found in the American literature on gangs. For Rhygin 'hard' equals 'heart'; for the other skinheads it equals ability and reputation.

3. The young women who associate with skinheads do not share a well-developed categorical identity (unlike the skinheads) but rather one based on personality and biography. Therefore, the personal and biographical bond which Jane shares with Tiffany and Debbie shapes her actions. I discuss this issue in more detail in Chapter Seven.

4. Danny did not come to Darcy's expressly to see Ace as he frequented that pub anyway.

5. The involvement of the bar staff and bouncers also has a commercial angle. The theme of Johnno's Bar is 1950s and the presence of the rockabillies added to the bar's overall ambience. The bar staff had also become friendly with many of the rockabillies because of their frequent attendance in past weeks. There was also a fair degree of anti-skinhead feeling amongst the bar security staff.

6. Horowitz and Schwartz (1974, p. 239) note the group nature of honour amongst Chicano gangs, 'In theory, derogation of one of their members affects their collective honor'.

7. Another example of violence within a single category is provided by the crocodile hunters of the Australian Northern Territory (Peter d'Abbs 1985, personal communication). There, fighting is limited to hitting above the belt and to using only one's fists to deliver blows. One reason for this informal restriction is that crocodile hunters tend to drink in the same regular venue and therefore the two protagonists may be drinking in the same place the following weekend. Serious injury could not be tolerated because it could spark long-term feuds in a small, tight-knit community.

5 Sociability and youth subcultures

At 7.30 p.m. on a Friday night, Rhygin and I enter Darcy's and meet several other skinheads. Through the evening we both see, and talk to, several people apart from the usual group. Those we encounter are mods, skinheads, ex-mods, ex-skinheads, teddy boys, rockabillies, and trendies. Superficially, these sets of people have nothing in common with one another stylistically. Neither do they have anything in common with Rhygin, except for the skinheads. One, Wilson, has been, at different periods in his stylistic career, a rude boy and a mod. He is presently a ted, resplendent in brothel creepers and drainpipe trousers, separated by lime-green socks. He wears a white shirt, Slim Jim tie and tailor-made drape coat. His assemblage is topped by his flamboyant quiff. Wilson visits Darcy's only occasionally, preferring either Johnno's Bar or organized 1950s nights. Another, Duncan, returned from a teenage visit to Scotland as a skinhead with 'no hair'. Later, he became a mod. He now dresses in a more mainstream style but still frequents the nightclub scene in general and, more specifically, the English scene. A third, Ron, is a public servant of four years' standing who has been, at varying stages, a skinhead, a mod, and a soul boy.

A typical evening in town included a series of such meetings in a series of venues, finding out what people had been 'up to', and the current state of their leisure lives. If the person is well known, and had been a good friend, inquiries into other domains of one's life might be made, perhaps about one's family or employment. But inquiries into one's leisure activities are far more common. What do these seemingly disparate persons have in common with one another and with Rhygin?

My primary aim in this chapter is to examine sociable interaction between members of different Perth youth subcultures comprising the English scene, although I also examine interaction with members of subcultures falling outside this field. My description complements the view given in the previous chapter, to ensure that the reader's impressions of skinhead violence do not blind him/her to the more sociable forms of interaction and to demonstrate how friendships are formed amidst this sociability. Rather than addressing the internal dynamics of the skinhead scene, I will attempt to make some more general points about the response of a section of youth to the urban environment. To paraphrase Hannerz (1980, p. 3), in this chapter the city is the focus rather than the locus of study. The chapter is a response to my ethnography as the sorts of encounters described above were initially puzzling to me. It is also directed to the literature and to a major criticism of the CCCS studies: that they portray youth subcultures as 'static and rigid anthropological entities' (Waters 1981).

In Britain, spectacular youth cultures periodically evolved out of preceding movements and, according to more recent publications (e.g., Redhead 1990), many of the earlier styles reappeared in the 1980s. Postwar youth styles are being reasserted yet the social conditions inspiring these reassertions are different from those which inspired the original genesis of these styles. Accounts of the nature of the relationship between members of different subcultures in recent times or in earlier periods are limited to generalized discussions of hostility and violence between groups such as hippies and skinheads (e.g., Hebdige 1979) and bikers and hippies (e.g., Willis 1978). Other authors see much violent interaction as a product of press distortion (e.g., S. Cohen 1980). As with the notion of style, a consideration of the performative aspects of these relationships is largely absent.

The context of sociability

If we were to believe the mass media, interaction between members of Perth youth subcultures supposedly runs according to a generalized 'we hate anybody not like us'. Undoubtedly there are those who subscribe to this ethos. However, some skinhead interaction with other English scene members, such as punks, teds or mods, is mediated by ties of friendship and knowledge of personal and/or subcultural identity running across subcultural boundaries. Persons gather bridging ties over a period of time invested in certain scenes and eras. Ties established by individuals are then aggregated to form a series of weak bridging ties within and across subcultural boundaries. The end result is a large pool of acquaintances, but a pool which differs from the quasi-group because its members are not candidates for recruitment for a specific purpose in the formation of action-sets. They form a dormant quasi-group made up of persons still known but not actively pursued. What these people have to say makes up part of the general information flow and the stories they may tell can mark one's involvement in past scenes and eras. The collecting of bridging ties is unintentional. Such ties are emergent products of one's authentic membership of scenes and eras.

This type of interaction occurs most at mixed venues, that is, those frequented by a cross-section of youth, but also at the regular skinhead venues. For example, for approximately three months over the Christmas-New Year period in 1982-3, Rhygin regularly visited an inner-city tavern patronized by members of the English scene. Wednesdays and Fridays were the most popular nights. Saturday patronage was confined to meeting others for a drink before going elsewhere. On Wednesday and Fridays, this tavern was well patronized and the clientele consisted of mods, some skinheads (those who conceded to the entry requirements), ex-skinheads, and others who did not fit comfortably into any of these categories but were nevertheless members of the English scene. During these three months, Rhygin met many people, all of them drinking, dancing and generally having a good time. He was an integral part of this scene until it lapsed as its members began seeking other establishments for their entertainment. However, eighteen months later, during my fieldwork, Rhygin saw several people he had met at this tavern and caught up with their activities. He also met people he had not previously known who had been part of that scene and era and became friendly with them because of this history of common participation. Despite many of them being mods, Rhygin still regarded them favourably and continues to see them in town. Although Rhygin voices his dislike of mods in general, many of his acquaintances have been, or are, mods. The link is the common experience of being members, albeit of different types, of the English scene, and in some cases of experiencing the same scenes and eras. The number of people known increases over years of subcultural involvement, whichever subculture one chooses, and the resulting experience of scenes and the participation in eras.

As a result of their patronage of pubs and other venues which are part of the English scene, skinheads rarely interact with members of youth subcultures which lie outside the parameters of this scene, for example, bogs or surfers. The venues chosen by skinheads (and other members of the English scene) rarely, if ever, include such persons in their clientele and skinheads rarely seek out venues which knowingly contain large numbers of them.

Despite this fact, knowledge of people across subcultural boundaries is not exclusively confined to the English scene. I witnessed several isolated instances when skinheads and bogs interacted, albeit briefly and in a superficial way (e.g., conversing on a city pavement). Rhygin disapproves of this interaction but he does not spend as much time in town during the day as the skinheads generally involved in this type of exchange. The link between the seemingly opposed groups was their common position – unemployed, marginal, bored youth spending time in the city – and the opportunity to exchange potentially important information about the constantly changing urban environment.

The source of sociability

In his book *Person, Time, and Conduct in Bali* (1966), Geertz explores the usefulness of separating the category of 'fellow-men' into predecessors, contemporaries, consociates, and successors, an idea first proposed by Schutz (1962). Using this breakdown allows us to examine the conceptions of personal identity, temporal order and behavioural style which are features of the interactions I have described above.

First to define these four terms. Consociates are persons who interact with one another continually, as opposed to occasionally, and for some lasting purpose in the course of their daily life. Thus consociates comprise the action-set and quasi-group discussed in Chapter Two. Contemporaries are persons sharing the same temporal dimension but who do not normally meet. The link between contemporaries lies in a widespread set of cultural assumptions about one another's typical modes of behaviour.[1] Predecessors and successors are, obviously, those persons who share neither a spatial nor a temporal dimension. The former, who may be known of, have already lived and their deeds may influence those who follow them. Successors cannot even be known of for they are the future generation but, as I have said, their behaviour may be influenced by the famous exploits of their predecessors.

In the original Schutzian scheme, little importance is placed on the transformative aspects of consociates, contemporaries, predecessors and successors. That is, how do people move back and forth between the various categories? While Geertz alludes to possible uses of these four categories in relation to time and space, and to the difficulty in separating the categories in everyday life, Schutz makes no mention of this relationship. For him, the concepts remain static. They are helpful for the discussion of skinhead relations with the members of other youth subcultures but their greatest potential lies in their ability to demystify the transformation of contemporary into consociate and vice-versa in the participation in scenes and eras.

For skinheads, and other members of the English scene, the division between consociates and contemporaries is hazy. Persons may move easily between the two categories in their social relationships with others. For example, in an earlier stylistic incarnation a mod may have been a skinhead and, through participation in scenes and eras with other skinheads, have built up a large quasi-group. Later, he becomes a mod and changes his immediate consociates accordingly. Some of his skinhead friends may change with him and also become mods, but he is also likely to retain ties with those who choose to remain skinheads. The switch is not usually complete unless made under hostile circumstances. Now his consociates consist of other mods and the former skinhead friends become contemporaries, still sharing a community of time but not of space. This knowledge of people within other subcultures may also derive from factors other than stylistic participation, that is, neighbourhood ties, contacts through female partners, and outside interests such as football. Those contemporaries who were close friends when consociates, could conceivably meet and become consociates again. The friendship may redevelop or be merely re-evoked in a fleeting conversation, 'What have you been up to?' The typical member of the English scene thus has his consociates, the quasi-group and more defined action-set, and a wide range of contemporaries who may always remain such or, alternatively, become consociates again at some later stage.

Not only members of other subcultures may be contemporaries. Other skinheads can be known of, through tales of their exploits, but not yet personally known. They are contemporaries who, in time, are likely to become consociates. Some of the older skinheads who are not yet personally known may never be known if they leave the skinhead scene. These older skinheads are predecessors to their successors, the skinheads presently making up the scene and those about to enter the scene in the near future. Stories of older skinheads and their exploits, or of those no longer skinheads, serve to shape conceptions about being a skinhead and 'what it was like in the old days' (even though 'the old days' may only refer to the last several years). Rhygin himself has proudly related instances where, on meeting a younger skinhead, the younger skinhead commented, 'I've heard of you'.

Due to lengthy participation in various scenes and eras, someone like Rhygin gains a large pool of contemporaries who have been past consociates. Apart from his present skinhead quasi-group, he can claim knowledge and the friendship of many mods, several teddy boys, trendies, and one or two punks, as well as several others who do not claim membership of any particular subculture. While these people are presently contemporaries, it will usually be only a matter of time before they meet and once again become consociates. The high frequency of meeting is due to the location of the English scene in a few sites at any one time. For those contemporaries who have never been consociates or predecessors, and are therefore unknown entities, resort is made to cultural assumptions about each other's typical modes of behaviour. Such assumptions form guides for the conduct of categorical relationships and explain the apparent contradiction in a statement like 'I hate mods!' when contrasted with the speaker's actions while talking with a known mod who is an ex-consociate.

Much of the discussion so far has dealt with the socialization into, and participation in, the skinhead subculture and English scene. When leaving this subculture (choosing to be 'out of it') a skinhead's former consociates, if they choose to continue their participation in the style, become contemporaries. Often a set will move out of the style together, its members thus remaining consociates as they adopt a new style together. They become predecessors to the next skinhead age grade, this following age grade being their successors. Sometimes, the skinhead will acquire new friends and leave the English scene completely.[2] The important point is that once a person ceases to be a skinhead, he can remain in the scene by adopting one of the other styles that comprise the English scene in Perth.

Contextualizing skinheads

The English scene then is a British youth community, many of whose members know one another through links built up over the years. This scene yields a social map of people comprising a large pool. Within the English scene, ethnicity and common experience of eras can mediate subcultural differences. Violence forcibly differentiates between groups, but sociability reasserts the commonality.

Waters (1981) criticizes the CCCS studies for focusing on the internal dynamics of subcultures at the expense of more sustained attention to the ever-changing relationships between subcultures and the larger society. In his view, subcultures are often viewed as closed anthropological entities – the mechanisms by which they function and are transformed are ignored. By showing the frequent transfer of personnel between subcultures comprising the English scene, through the transformative aspect of Schutz's contemporaries and consociates, I have illustrated the relationship between the skinhead subculture and its immediate social context. Perth skinheads cannot be separated in analysis from members of the English scene nor from the wider youth contexts in which they move.

Notes

1. Here Geertz is reworking the notion of categorical relationships which Mitchell drew from Wirth, 'categorical relationships ... arise in any situation where contacts must of necessity be fleeting and transitory' (Mitchell 1956, p. 29).

2. An excellent account of the processes involved in a total switch of consociates can be found in Hill (1974). Although the context is different the described processes of changing one's consociates are remarkably similar.

6 Drinking and the construction of ethnicity

One of the ways in which skinheads choose to construct and express their ethnic identity is in their patterns of drinking.[1] Moreover, these drinking patterns also constitute some of the underlying social processes which characterize interaction within this subculture and with members of other youth subcultures.

Burke's (1945) dramaturgical perspective provides an appropriate framework for the analysis of skinhead drinking. To understand human modes of action he argues that the same 'act', in this case drinking, takes on different forms and meanings in different 'scenes' (i.e., 'settings') because the nature of the act and the agents (the 'actors') must be consistent with the scene. In other words, the scene contains both the act and the agent. Having a quiet drink with a friend at home or at the local pub is vastly different from heavy drinking with several friends in an inner-city nightclub on a Friday night. While drinking is entailed in most skinhead group activity, it assumes different forms which are defined by the situation at hand. Therefore, in Burkian terms, we may say that an agent is constrained to drink heavily in a scene which requires high levels of consumption. The combination of skinhead (the agent), drinking (the act), and a night in the city (the scene) produces a known style of action.

Skinhead drinking style

Let us suppose that a skinhead has money and a party of consociate skinheads ready and willing to embark on a drinking venture. What happens? The organization and style of skinhead drinking takes two basic forms depending on the social context. To help illustrate the differences between these two forms, what follows is an ethnographic excerpt which illustrates a drinking session on a typical Friday night.

I enter Darcy's with Rhygin at about 7.30 p.m. As arranged, we meet Ace, Nutter, Terry, Scouse, and the others. After the initial mock-abusive greetings and assorted comments about one's dress, hair, and general demeanour, Rhygin and I move to the bar to order drinks while others replenish their pint glasses. Other skinheads are already paired into drinking partners – Ace and Nutter, Scouse and Tiny, Terry and Smithy. Rhygin turns to the bar attendant and, on gaining her attention, calls, 'Two pints'. One of the explicit reasons given by Rhygin for arriving at the pub at this early time (early when one considers how long the night will continue, possibly until 3 or 4 a.m.) is to ensure that 'there're still some pint glasses left'. Likewise, if for some reason a pair's arrival at the pub is delayed, one of the incentives is that 'We'll have to hurry or there'll be no pint glasses left'.

On gaining our drinks, we join the rough circle of lads each clutching the precious pint 'pot'. The abusive banter which had greeted our arrival and been returned now resumes. Others, some in pairs, some in threes, others alone, arrive to run the gauntlet of the abusive arrival routine. They too make for the bar and hurriedly secure pint glasses. Stories are exchanged and relevant information imparted about gender relationships, recent fights, someone's recent court appearance, relaxed entry requirements at a nightclub, a party the following Saturday night. We discuss the availability of pint glasses as one of the criteria in a positive evaluation of a particular pub. A latecomer arrives and joins the set holding a middy glass (285 ml). He confides to me, 'I hate drinking out o' these'. Rhygin visits the toilet, leaving his pint glass in my care to be reclaimed afterwards. I notice that Ace, Nutter, Scouse, and other skinheads also follow this practice when leaving the drinking area for any reason.

Our collective attention is drawn to a scuffle which has broken out on the far side of the bar. As is typical in fights inside crowded bars, the first sign is the crush of people trying to move out of danger of flying fists. This creates a ripple effect which spreads away from the violent epicentre. Someone brings news that another skinhead has become embroiled in a scuffle with a stranger. The skinhead and his opponent have both been ejected from the bar. Several skinheads follow outside to aid in exacting physical revenge from the stranger for the initial assault. Those involved in the fight are forced to leave the immediate area by the imminent arrival of the police.

The rest of us remain inside the bar drinking. Several pints later, the decision is made by one pair to leave and seek entertainment elsewhere. They finish their drinks and head off into the night. Other skinheads arrive, having been delayed by work, a car problem, a meeting with a girlfriend. The night wears on. At midnight, the pub closes and those who wish to continue drinking are forced to consider their options. Some elect to go home, a decision sometimes based on financial constraints. Others choose a certain nightclub. One pair decides against this choice and opts to visit an alternative venue. One skinhead has been fortunate enough to gain an invitation to spend the rest of the evening with a newly-acquired female acquaintance.

We regroup in one of the nightclubs. The drinking continues but no longer are pint glasses an option. Nobody really cares by now.

The pattern of events described in this excerpt are common to most evenings spent in town. The significance placed on gaining and retaining the pint-sized drinking vessel, the drinking in pairs or individually, the emphasis on heavy drinking, and the intermittent nature of arrival and exit from the drinking venue all define the skinhead style of drinking in the evening context.

This heavy drinking night style often provides the context for interpersonal violence as well as the opportunity for the expression of ethnic identity. This form usually involves large numbers, both of skinheads and other youth, in inner-city hotels, bars and nightclubs. The drinking begins between 7 and 8 p.m. and continues relatively unabated until the early hours of the morning. The amount drunk obviously depends on the particular person but will probably vary between four and ten pints. The evening usually begins at a favourite hotel where one meets other skinheads and friends. Drinks are also cheaper in these establishments than in late-licence nightclubs, so one of the aims is to get a few drinks under one's belt before venturing elsewhere. One reason for choosing a particular hotel is the availability of pint glasses. Another is musical taste. For several years, the location of the English scene in Perth followed a limited number of disc jockeys from venue to venue because of the latest English music they chose to play.

By about midnight (and sometimes earlier) most, if not all, the skinheads are in fairly advanced states of intoxication, either 'pissed', 'rotten pissed', or the more extreme 'legless'. However, a particular nightclub is often nominated and those with sufficient stamina and money move on to drink elsewhere, usually on foot due to the relative closeness of Perth's inner-city licensed venues. The fact that this form of subcultural expression occurs most in this sphere relates to its more public nature. That is, drinking in town on a Friday evening provides more chance for interaction with other youth (and the public in general), both with members of other recognized subcultures and those not so obviously aligned.

Although one of the reasons skinheads give for drinking is to 'get pissed' and to experience alcohol's physiological effects, it should also be recognized that heavy consumption within a pub/nightclub context is seen as normal. Remaining sober and visiting a nightclub are seen as antithetical activities and those that do so are regarded with what borders on disbelief. To the skinhead, visiting the city at night and heavy drinking to intoxication are related parts of the same context.

Like the above account, what follows is an ethnographic sketch of a somewhat different form of drinking session. One Wednesday lunchtime, Rhygin and I drive to meet Ace and Nutter at Ace's house. We decide to visit the local pub and while away a few hours of the afternoon drinking and playing pool. On the way we call at Scouse's residence and he agrees to join us. We arrive at the pub, enter the public bar and order our drinks. Rhygin and I buy in a pair, Nutter buys for Scouse (who has no money), Ace buys his own. We settle into a doubles game of pool with Scouse, not noted for his pool-playing ability, looking on. The bar contains the usual smattering of daytime regulars, mostly older, retired men with a smattering of younger drinkers.

Rhygin and I win the first game, much to Ace and Nutter's chagrin, and then Scouse is called upon to play a singles game against Nutter. Scouse's obvious lack of finesse provides Ace, Nutter, Rhygin and me with considerable entertainment. Nutter ends up doubled over with laughter at the sight of Scouse's inability to judge the necessary angles required to pot any balls and his frustration at not being able to match the others' skills.

Ace rings Tiny from the public phone in the bar. He invites him to join us at the pub and share in the spectacle of Scouse's pool technique. However, Tiny excuses himself on the grounds of a planned rendezvous with a young woman at his house while his parents are at work. After several crude innuendoes Ace allows Tiny to end the phone conversation to await his visitor. Returning to our group, Ace suggests that we might visit Tiny later to verify the truthfulness of his excuse and to evaluate the young woman's attractiveness should it prove correct.

The pool challenges continue as does the drinking at a sedate pace for a couple of hours. Finally we leave the pub as Ace wants to eat before readying himself for his evening's football training with a local team. However, on the way back to Ace's, we call at Tiny's house to find his excuse justified on several counts. With our curiosity satisfied, Rhygin and I drop Ace, Nutter and Scouse off at their respective houses and drive home.

The points to note in this second account are the small number of skinhead personnel involved, the leisurely pace of drinking and associated activities, the location of activity in a local pub rather than the more public inner city, and the absence of the features described in the first extract and generally associated with skinheads, that is, fighting, heavy drinking to intoxication, and behaviour usually labelled as rowdy and troublesome by the general public.

Downing a couple of pints or middies in a suburban hotel on a quiet midweek afternoon is a very different order of drinking to a Friday night drinking session in various inner-city pubs and night-clubs. The former is more likely to be a relatively restrained affair centred around a pool table or a quiet drink at the bar. Occasionally, this more sedate form of drinking may assume some of the charact-eristics of the heavy drinking sessions. There may be a special reason to celebrate (e.g., a birthday), several more skinheads may arrive unexpectedly, or the session may take on this form due to the social forces arising out of interaction among those present. This latter reason depends to a great extent on the identities of the drinking personnel. If some members of the group are of exuberant, flamboyant character, the quiet afternoon may turn into a fully-fledged 'piss-up' often continuing into the night or until funds have been exhausted. The achievement of this evolution from the light to the heavy drinking form in a spontaneous fashion is much prized and is structurally facilitated by the minimal planning of such drinking occasions.

If any form of round drinking ever takes place among skinheads, it usually occurs in the daytime setting. This occurs because the emphasis on ease of movement, so important to the night style, is absent from this time. Those settling in for a few afternoon games of pool and a few drinks are unlikely to want to dash off to another pub. This diluted form of round drinking does not have explicit rules and is grounded in specific personal relationships.

Common to the above accounts is the skinhead choice of beer as the preferred alcoholic beverage. In most Perth pubs, if one asks for a 'middy' one receives lager (with an alcohol content of approximately five per cent for full-strength beer). While beer is the most popular drink, skinheads also drink spirits on occasions. Because of the greater cost of spirits the choice of beer is often dictated by financial considerations. One practice aimed at circumventing this prohibitive cost is to smuggle a small bottle of, say, whisky, onto licensed premises. Once safely inside, the bottle's possessor buys Coca-Cola or some other mixer and pours some of the whisky into the mixer either under the table or in some other discreet fashion. The comparison on, say, twelve drinks, is that the cost of spirits is reduced to about one-half of the bar price. If the bottle of whisky is stolen (rather than bought) prior to entering licensed premises, the cost is further reduced to about one-quarter of the bar price. Once the supply of illicit spirit is exhausted a switch is made to purchasing beer. Another practice for gaining cheap, highly-alcoholic beverages is to plan a shoplifting venture at a bottleshop (a drive-in liquor store attached to a pub) or a liquor store (an off-licence). While one skinhead, or possibly several (and sometimes females), occupies the attention of the staff, another person will conceal a bottle of whisky or some other spirit and leave the premises without payment. In these two ways, one guarantees relatively inexpensive alcoholic drinks until the spirit runs out.

Like many young people, the quantity a skinhead drinks on any one occasion and the frequency of the drinking sessions in an average week vary according to a number of factors. If he is currently unemployed, his effective buying power is limited. He may decide to drink more but on fewer occasions during the week or drink less on more occasions. The former is the more popular choice with money being saved for Friday and Saturday nights' drinking. If he is currently or recently employed, and has managed to save some money, the drinking on Friday and Saturday nights is likely to be accompanied by Sunday afternoon/evening and midweek, often daytime, drinking.

However, the most significant factor affecting the quantity/-frequency ratio is the availability of consociate skinhead drinkers. A skinhead may have money to spend on drinking but if his usual drinking partners are 'skint' or unable or unwilling to purchase drinks for other reasons (e.g., dedicating the money to some other purpose) he will rarely drink alone. Drinking is done in a group setting and highly valued as an aid to sociability. If the skinhead has little money but is invited to join a potential drinking party, he may still accept knowing that his drinking level may fall well below that of the others (if they have money). He will still accept because he does not want to miss out on the action; some excitement may be generated by the drinking party during their outing. Another possibility is for one or more of those with money to allocate some of their money to purchasing him drinks. However, there is no ethos of generalized reciprocity whereby one skinhead will buy drinks for another in the expectation that the favour will be returned at some future stage. The buying of drinks for another is relatively rare given the amount of time spent drinking and usually belongs to a specific relationship grounded in intertwining biographies, extraordinary past events (often fights where aid was rendered), or between close friends.

The responses of particular skinheads to drunkenness may be predicted by personalities. For example, one skinhead who is part-icularly amiable and gregarious becomes even more so when drunk. Another, a more cynical and aggressive character, likewise empha-sizes these traits when intoxicated. However, as one would expect from past research into the effects of alcohol (e.g., MacAndrew and Edgerton 1969), the drunken demeanour of skinheads is also largely shaped by situational circumstances. Being 'with the lads', hearing one's favourite songs, generally larking around, and possibly spying a young woman who takes one's fancy all contribute to a sometimes euphoric mood. At the threat of danger, individually and collectively, more aggressive stances are adopted which may lead to violence.

The announcement of ethnicity

The influence of ethnicity on the formation of drinking styles has been well documented in the sociological literature (e.g., Bennet and Ames 1985). Likewise, skinhead drinking is 'formed in part as a reaction or in reference to other ethnicities' (Room 1985, p. xv) and contrasts sharply with that of the Australian moidy stereotype. A feature of Australian writings on drinking is the description of the male 'shout' which is held to symbolize egalitarianism expressed through the structure of drinking.[2] Beer is bought in jugs (1136 ml) and then poured into middy glasses held by each drinker. Each drinker in turn 'shouts' (buys) a jug and redistributes its contents to the others in the drinking party. In this way all contribute financially to the drinking session and reaffirm the equality of status of those involved. As Kapferer (1988, p. 159) states:

> The shout places all the drinkers into equivalent relation, regardless of social or economic position. Indeed, the shout facilitates the formation of drinking groups that cuts across the social differentiation of the outside world. A person can enter a group on a more or less immediate understanding that he will

participate in its life on an equal footing. The shout creates equality and contributes to the marked disposition of Australian drinking groups to encompass persons of different social and economic backgrounds and positions of power in society. The shout is actively antagonistic to distinction – as is Australian egalitarianism as a whole – and in the practice of it there is pressure to resist differentiating factors or else to refuse actively to recognize their emergence should they intrude.

In the cultural constructions of skinheads, the moidy conforms to this widely recognized Australian pattern and drinks in shouts, often being seen in the public bars that skinheads frequent. Skinheads avoid drinking in this shouting pattern not to avoid any identification with the moidy, for there would be little chance of that occurring given the enormous differences in clothing and hairstyles, but because to drink in this way is seen to be 'Australian' while being a skinhead is about being, or at least appearing to be, English. Whatever the actual importance of shouting for regulating and ordering the drinking behaviour of groups of Australian males, Perth skinheads are aware of this pattern (especially the structure built around the purchasing of jugs) and incorporate it into their explicit and named stereotype of the moidy. It remains a cultural pattern recognized in skinhead perceptions and by many Australians, as evidenced in the phrases one commonly hears in pubs, 'Your shout', 'It's my shout', and the less flattering (and particularly Australian) 'He wouldn't shout if a shark bit 'im'.

To announce their ethnicity, skinheads employ a variety of measures which I have detailed in earlier chapters – clothing incorporating the Union Jack or other obviously English motifs as well as components of a style that is recognized as English by other youth (e.g., Doc Marten boots, retention, exaggeration or invention of English accents, pro-English tattoos). The skinheads are aided in this by the fact that many Perth residents are familiar with this youth style through media reports, both about local and English skinheads, and associate it with England. The measure that relates to drinking is consumption of beer in pints.

In Western Australia, traditional measures for the drinking of beer include the jug (1136 ml), schooner (425 ml), the middy (285 ml), the glass (200 ml) and the pony (140 ml) (these sizes vary across Australia). Most Perth pubs serve beer in these measures. Some, for a variety of reasons (as a marketing ploy to a largely British clientele or as part of a burgeoning designer beer movement), also offer the option of pint measures. Many of the pubs that skinheads frequent

offer this latter alternative. In the minds of mai
Perth at least, drinking in pints or half-pints is
Britain. More importantly, skinheads perceive drii
and shouting as being a characteristically Australiai
drinking from pint glasses is seen as being an Engli:
alongside other measures for the announcement of
ethnicity, and their rejection of all that is overtly
skinheads drink in pints wherever possible.[3]

The sociology of skinhead drinking

In their discussion of drinking in an East Anglian village, Hunt and
Satterlee (1983) outline several reasons why the local, predominantly
working-class residents of the village do not drink in rounds whereas
the middle-class residents do. Their thesis is that the locals in the
village have little need to establish membership of a group because
they are already heavily enmeshed in networks of kinship and
neighbourhood. The middle-class drinkers (relatively recent arrivals
in the village due to rural immigration) who drink almost exclusively
in rounds do so as a means of establishing common status and
membership in a group. Their discussion raises several general
criteria for the establishment of the practice of round drinking:
similar status (or the pretence of similar status) between
participating individuals, a notion of reciprocity or stored credit,
sufficient disposable income, a willingness to create and later
discharge obligation, a need to enhance group cohesion because of a
lack of categorical identity, and the need to affirm membership status
in the group. These criteria have important implications for the
sociology of non-round drinking amongst skinheads, and amongst
the members of other youth groups.

By having one's hair shorn, donning Doc Marten boots and
investing time and resources in being with other skinheads, one
establishes membership of the category. The skinhead does not need
to join a drinking round to establish this membership; it is already
established by act of declaring himself a skinhead, adopting skinhead
garb and, more importantly, being accorded this status by other
skinheads. Even more so, being a skinhead is about 'standing with
yer mates' in violent situations so there is little need to further
cement this status through round drinking, especially given the
financial limitations of most skinheads.

Hunt and Satterlee also note the need for equality of status.
According to descriptions of the Australian shout and of round
drinking procedures in general, those involved in the round must

...ny notions of hierarchy to preserve the egalitarianism of ...nd. While skinheads do not have a formal hierarchy they do ...e self-liquidating positions or identities which are created by the actions of persons and the collective judgements brought down on these actions by other skinheads. In other words, one's position in the achieved status hierarchy in relation to other skinheads is important and is unlikely to be suspended in deference to drinking. A skinhead with a sizeable reputation for toughness is unlikely to be prepared to spend scarce resources on a subcultural novice of little note.

As I mentioned earlier, there is no ethos of generalized reciprocity in the skinhead subculture which would allow a stored credit system. There is little willingness on the part of most skinheads to create obligations that they might later be unable or unwilling to meet. One cannot guarantee that drinks purchased at one point will be returned in the future. Perhaps more importantly, buying drinks for others has little relevance to claiming the identity 'skinhead'; whether or not one buys drinks for others is of minimal importance.

The drinking style also reflects financial considerations whereby a skinhead, by virtue of unemployment or low-paid employment, allocates a set amount of money for an evening's drinking. He can rarely afford to become involved in round drinking and possibly spend a large percentage of the money with little guarantee of reciprocity at some later stage in the evening. If involved in round drinking, with this possibility of uneven expenditure, his funds may be exhausted before reaching the desired state of intoxication. Even on those occasions or during those periods when skinheads have money, round drinking is not entered into for the reasons presented above. Financial limitations are probably a feature not only of skinhead drinking patterns but also of most other youth social collectivities.

A final reason for the absence of round drinking is the social organization of the skinhead subculture. Skinhead drinking patterns reflect the locating of specific activity in action-sets. One recruits, or rather joins, an action set for a potential 'good night' which involves heavy drinking. Rather than shouting one another rounds of drinks in the usual Australian fashion, skinheads usually drink in pairs or individually. This pattern means that any pair or person can arrive or leave at any time and not upset the drinking rhythm. This social feature contrasts with one of the central findings of the Barbara, Usher and Barnes (1978, p. 126) study of shouting; that 'the most significant public act that destroys group solidarity is leaving the group at an inappropriate time'. Should two skinheads announce that they are leaving one pub to meet friends at another or choose to leave one set within a pub and join another, they are not called upon to wait and finish the round of group drinking before leaving. In this way a pair is not restricted in its movements by a group round of perhaps four or five people. The practice of round drinking is avoided because it is not suited to the dynamics of skinhead social organization.

Does the skinhead practice of non-round drinking reflect an English style which has been transported, along with other aspects of being English, to Perth? Wilson (1980, p. 16) states that, for England and Wales, approximately fifty per cent of men's and fifty-nine per cent of women's drinking occasions take place in groups of three or more (when in pubs). Dennis, Henriques and Slaughter (1956) report round drinking amongst working-class coal miners as does Dorn (1983) for working-class youth in the service sector, while Hunt and Satterlee (1983) examine a well-developed round drinking style amongst a new rural middle class. The drinking style of Perth skinheads more closely resembles that of the local working-class people also reported by Hunt and Satterlee, although for slightly different reasons. It is clear from this literature that there is no single English drinking style and that the existence of round drinking depends on a wide range of factors. The skinhead drinking style is not a mere transplant of a peculiarly English style but one which owes its genesis and maintenance to unique social processes of ethnic differentiation and subcultural form. In stark contrast to the cultural milieu in which they find themselves, Perth skinheads choose to drink in a manner which establishes their English ethnicity and reflects the social processes constituting their expressive activity. In their drinking behaviour, Perth skinheads give the lie to the Australian context in which they find themselves.

Notes

1. A version of this chapter has been published elsewhere (Moore 1990).

2. For discussions of Australian 'shouting', see Barbara, Usher and Barnes (1978), Conway (1971), Fiske, Hodge and Turner (1987), Horne (1964), McGregor (1967), Oxley (1978), Sargent (1973), and Ward (1966). For a fictional treatment of Australian drinking, see Ireland (1982). I am particularly indebted to Philip Moore for his ethnographic observations about shouting amongst building subcontractors in Perth (P. Moore 1991).

7 Skinhead relationships with young women

Who needs birds. Birds are for when you want to get married.

(Paul in general conversation)

You've got a boyfriend who cares the world for you.

(Ace chastising Carol over her treatment of Paul)

A great deal of skinhead group discussion is given over to the subject of relationships with women.[1] If the relationship is, or was, of a casual and/or short-lived nature this discussion often focuses on the sexual aspects of the relationship. Discussions about relationships with regular female partners are considerably more reticent, particularly for the duration of the liaison. The tone of the discussion is also affected by the social context in which it takes place – the identity of the narrator, the size and composition of the audience, and the site of the discussion. The tone of storytelling to an audience of four or five skinheads after the consumption of several drinks is markedly different to that characterizing a conversation between two friends over a cup of tea. I deal with public discussions, that is, those involving at least two or three persons and usually occurring in a pub or other public leisure setting. It is in these settings that the skinhead fashions his public sexual self.

The public representation of the sexual self

Skinheads claim to be exploiters of young women, primarily for sex, and presume that all men perceive young women in the same way; it is a taken-for-granted view of such relationships, as the following example demonstrates.[2] One afternoon, several skinheads and I were drinking and playing pool in a suburban pub. One skinhead related a recent escapade when he and another skinhead had 'picked up two birds', taken them back to a friend's house and had sex with them. He conceded that his partner was 'ugly but good in bed' (in this context he meant compliant). The storyteller's verdict was that even though the woman was judged to be physically unattractive, 'a fuck's a fuck'.

On another occasion Jack, Roy, Nutter, Rhygin, Ace, Terry, Rachel and I had stopped in a car park just outside Perth (we had been travelling in two cars) to decide the agenda for the rest of the evening's activities. We had been unable to find the party for which we had been searching. Ace expressed a desire to go somewhere where there were 'birds'. He felt confident that he could 'chat up some birds' and bring them back to Paul and Carol's flat for a party. His suggestion sparked a chorus of disagreement from the others about its reality and about his ability to successfully complete the task he had set himself. Ace himself recognized the fantasy of his suggestion but continued the theme for its entertainment value. One of the set ridiculed Ace for having 'had' (had sex with) a young woman thought to be a 'bush pig' (a young woman considered very 'ugly'), earlier in the week. Jack began stirring Ace over this union. He said that although he had slept with another young woman also widely regarded as a 'bush pig', he would not stoop to sex with Ace's partner. Ace's axiomatic and dismissive reply was, 'I get my fucks, mate!'

Not all skinheads are equally successful at 'pulling birds' for a variety of reasons, such as physical appearance, the failure to establish a subcultural reputation, or a lack of dress sense, confidence or wit. Therefore, as well as discussing sexual encounters and their various dimensions, much of the talk also revolves around one's failure to 'pick up a bird' and the art of (not) doing so. 'Chatting up birds' has expressive and instrumental dimensions. The artistic component has entertainment value; it is proof of one's nerve and wit and provides the substance for much conversation. Instrumentally, this practice, if successful, gains the skinhead access to sexual activity and by virtue of this, a reputation as someone who can 'pull the birds' or who 'gets his fucks'.

An analysis of skinhead conversations also suggests that fidelity to one's current partner is not highly valued. Skinheads who are currently recognized to be the 'boyfriends' of particular young women represent themselves as feeling little compunction about availing themselves of casual sex with other females, should the opportunity arise. In fact, there is considerable pressure to create these opportunities. For several weeks, Roy had an affair with a young woman via a series of nightclub rendezvous while continuing his steady relationship with Karen. Although ultimately failing, Tom attempted to 'pull' a young woman he met in Darcy's while 'seeing' (being in a relationship with) another young woman. His representation of the event left one in no doubt of his dismissal of the need for fidelity .

The story of Billy provides a case of infidelity celebrated by skin-heads. Billy had been 'going out with' Michelle for a number of weeks. However, after one eventful Saturday evening at a nightclub, Billy had sex with another young woman, Kate. In the conversation about this event, which spanned several weeks, much of the talk focused on the sexual aspects of the encounter. Details of the unusual setting for the sexual act, a discussion of the sexual history of the young woman involved (with respect to other skinheads), and broad details about the physical aspects of the encounter, as well as the need to conceal the encounter from Michelle, all drew responses, approval and laughter from a variety of assembled male audiences. Billy gained a considerable amount of prestige, although his identity as someone with a penchant for the unusual was already well on its way to being crafted prior to the incident. The consensus of the set was that, at least for matters sexual, he should 'take the cake' in my study for his unusual and numerous exploits.

There is also considerable derision for the skinhead who fails to pursue such opportunities for casual sex with someone other than a regular partner. Rhygin and Nutter were standing in a nightclub watching the dance floor and drinking. Other members of the skinhead set were adrift elsewhere within the club. A young woman described by both Nutter and Rhygin as 'really nice' approached Nutter for a light for her cigarette. He obliged. In Rhygin's depiction, she then smiled and lingered a moment longer than would normally be expected. She turned her back on Nutter but did not move away, standing in front of him smoking her cigarette. Rhygin asked Nutter if he knew her because, in his eyes, her movements indicated a certain approachability and openness. Nutter did not. Rhygin suggested a course of action, signalled in the deafeningly noisy nightclub by holding out a bent, upturned arm and a clenched fist and moving it in an upward motion. Nutter watched her for a while until she moved away. His chance was lost.

Rhygin, and the other skinheads who later heard the story, felt Nutter had wasted an opportunity to initiate discussion with the young woman. Nutter defended himself against their charge that he lacked nerve with the explanation that his current 'bird' was nearby in the nightclub and may have materialized at any moment. Rhygin would not accept this feeble excuse stating that 'it was a fucking waste' and that 'you should have made more of it'. Rhygin and the other skinheads expressed the opinion that Nutter should have acted to initiate proceedings with the young woman. They were announcing the group ideology: never refuse the chance to 'chat up a bird'. Nutter's excuse, the proximity of his partner, failed to strike a resonant chord in the others.

The emphasis in the public representation of these encounters is on sex, or at least the pursuit of sex, rather than the establishment and maintenance of other aspects of a new relationship with a woman. The skinhead is ordinarily portrayed as a seeker and taker of sex with little emotional attachment and the search for sex is represented as a focal concern. The archetypal skinhead 'pulls the birds' and 'gets his fucks'. Stories about such encounters contribute to folk knowledge and help to shape attitudes to future encounters. The all-male nature of these discussions means that young women do not have the opportunity to correct or question this carefully nurtured social image (just as males do not have access to the conversations of females). While it would be hasty to discount the lads' view of themselves entirely, this public representation only partly describes the nature of skinhead relationships with young women.

The complication of emotional involvement

In the previous section, I detailed the public representation of Billy's infidelity with Kate while maintaining a relationship with Michelle. In the postmortem on this event, Billy had been congratulated on his actions and had accepted this public version of himself as an exploiter of women. However, his private version of the night's events is somewhat different and more complex. He had found himself with the chance to have sex with another young woman, Kate. Although he professed to care for Michelle, he felt confused, unsure of whether or not to pursue this opportunity. He asked Ace, Nutter and Rhygin what he should do. Their initial response was that he should have sex with Kate that night and then leave her in the morning. Billy was still undecided. He elected to transfer the responsibility for a decision to Kate by informing her of his relationship with Michelle. This news did not alter Kate's feelings (in Billy's words, 'She had been hanging round my neck all night'). His conscience apparently clear, Billy decided to follow the advice of the other skinheads. However, moments before leaving, Nutter relayed a message from Rachel to Billy. Apparently, Michelle had confided to Rachel that she 'really liked' Billy and Rachel's advice to Nutter was to prevent Billy from 'messing up' the relationship. Nutter's final words were, 'Remember you've got a girl waiting for you at home'. Even as the taxi moved slowly away from the kerb with the others inside, Billy said he thought of leaving, but finally decided to press on with the tryst.

About two weeks later, in what appears to be a contradiction given this recent infidelity, Billy felt that Michelle's feelings for him were waning. One Saturday night, partially as a result of his insecurities over the state of his relationship with Michelle, Billy had engaged in the vandalizing of a garden fence by diving bodily through the pickets, smashing them into a pile of splintered wood. Later in the evening, as the set walked across the car park of a suburban shopping centre, Billy's fears were confirmed. Michelle took him aside from the rest of the set and told him she wanted to end their relationship but hoped that they could remain friends. Billy wheeled away, crying, 'Fuck off!' when she attempted to restrain him. He strode away from the group to lean against the window of a nearby fast-food establishment. One of the other young women tried to console him. While conversing with her, Billy overheard Rhygin yelling at Michelle that she had upset Billy. Rhygin's tirade stimulated Billy to action and he began kicking and punching the window he had been leaning against. He then sprinted across the car park to a six-foot-high Good Samaritans bin (for the collection of second-hand clothing for charity), kicked it over, and then turned his attentions to a shopping trolley and some stacked bread crates, hurling them around him in a frenetic display of anger and emotion. He spied Michelle walking to a telephone booth and reached her as she moved inside it. He began demanding that she reveal her reasons for ending their relationship. Michelle remained silent. Karen and Jane joined them in an effort to relieve the tension and perhaps also to ensure that Billy did not strike Michelle. Spent from his physical efforts, Billy's anger subsided. Two taxis were called and the set journeyed into the city to continue the night's activities in a nightclub.

On several other occasions during my fieldwork, I witnessed incidents which were related to, and expressive of, emotional attachments with young women, and which sometimes involved instances of wilful vandalism, self-mutilation, and other forms of self-directed violence or disregard for danger. Prior to her relationship with Billy, Michelle had been involved with another skinhead, Paul. On several occasions Paul stated that on splitting up with Michelle he had taken a glass to his own forehead and cut

107

himself several times. Other skinheads had witnessed this act and his forehead still bore the scars. To me, this action was all the more extraordinary when one considered Paul's normally phlegmatic character. Yet those who had witnessed the original act saw nothing ridiculous or eccentric in his actions. In fact, some skinheads expressed privately their admiration for Paul's scars.

Perhaps the most dramatic incident of the expression of emotion occurred towards the end of a night at an inner-city hotel. Throughout the evening, Pete and Karen had been arguing, a fairly common occurrence. Rhygin, Terry and I were standing in a bar close to the entrance to the hotel. The others were scattered throughout the lounge bar or playing pool in the public bar. We heard and then saw a commotion. First Karen and then Pete were escorted forcibly to the door by bouncers. Ace appeared out of the crowd and whispered something to Rhygin. They both hurriedly followed Pete, Karen and the bouncers down the passage, out of the door and onto the footpath outside. I also followed and arrived on the pavement amidst a small crowd of perhaps a dozen onlookers including some mods, who did not know Pete personally, and the skinheads who had been playing pool in the public bar, who knew Pete well.

Pete and Karen were arguing violently with Pete being restrained by Ace. I overheard one of the spectators say that Pete had 'nutted a boong'. This was feasible given the forty or so Aborigines standing about thirty yards up the pavement and across the road, who were taking an increasing interest in the pavement altercation. Pete broke free of Ace's hold on him and lurched into the road to be struck a glancing blow by a slow-moving taxi. Ace and Rhygin raced onto the road to pick him up. Ace tried to calm Pete down but he continued yelling and screaming. He tore himself away from Ace and rushed back towards Karen only to pass her and begin head-butting a shop window. I waited for the window to shatter after each thudding blow. Pete turned to Karen and the gathered onlookers and cried, 'I'm hard, see. That's how fucking hard I am!' Not finished, Pete turned to a nearby car and began booting the door, moving along the row to a second, a third and then a fourth car, repeating the treatment for successive doors and wing mirrors. Karen followed and began arguing with him again. She began punching and striking him with her handbag. Pete swayed but stayed on his feet, weakly trying to protect himself but making no attempt to fight back. I thought at this stage that he appeared dazed and near collapse. However, he snapped out of his trance and, crouching at the nearest parking meter, began butting it with his forehead with great force.

After five or six butts, he stood, whirled back towards the growing and incredulous crowd, blood coursing in rivulets over his contorted face, clenched his fist and screamed hysterically, 'Come on, let's have some aggro!'

His intentions declared, he spun away and lurched up the street. He paused to kick yet another car, kicked over two bicycles chained to a post, and swung his jacket at an old man walking towards him, before crossing the road about forty yards away and disappearing around a corner. Across the road the large contingent of Aborigines began moving slowly in the same direction. Roy, Karen, and some of the other skinheads also began to pursue Pete who, although out of sight, could still be heard screaming. Ace and Rhygin, simultaneously surprised and annoyed by Pete's outburst but more so about Karen's alleged stirring of Pete, walked back into the hotel to order more drinks.

The response to this incident was twofold. The crowd did not disperse for some moments afterwards and I was able to listen to a number of the immediate analyses. Those who did not personally know Pete and Karen felt Pete's actions to be bordering on the farcical, particularly the failed attempt to smash the shop window by head-butting it. In their opinion, it was all plain stupidity. However, in the eyes of Rhygin, Ace, Terry, and several others who witnessed the scene and who knew the biography of Pete and Karen, Pete's actions were explicable in the context of that relationship and in the more general context of all relationships between men and women. Their responses, while tinged with rebuke, were largely sympathetic and understanding. Ace's response was an angry one because the incident was yet another in the litany of disagreements between the two. But it was not an anger based on incomprehension. Pete, rightly or wrongly, was assessed to have behaved in such a way as a direct result of his repeated arguments with Karen and of his strong feelings for her. This belief was shared by other skinheads. It was understood that men could behave this way in response to emotions aroused as a result of matters of the heart, and that Pete had expressed them in an extreme but acceptable manner. Rhygin perhaps summarized this opinion when he said, 'I hope I never get like that over a girl'.

The resolution of public representation and private action

We have two vastly different and apparently contradictory modes of behaviour centring on young women; put simply, skinhead as exploiter and 'puller of birds' and skinhead as emotionally charged young man. A clue to the reconciliation of these competing modes is provided by Liebow (1967), in discussing the African American streetcorner men of Washington and their dealings with women. He suggests that there are two modes of accommodation in African American man/woman relationships – the ideal and the real. His streetcorner men also represent a public fiction concerning their exploitative view of women, yet their actions do not always tally with these pronouncements. Liebow concludes that in the ideal mode these men separate sexual and financial opportunism from feelings based on intimacy whereas in the real mode any given relationship combines aspects of both. For the African American men he studied the ideal distinction is reflected in the division of women into 'nice' and 'not nice'. The not-nice women are to be exploited whereas the nice woman warrants a more considerate relationship.

Likewise, Perth skinheads divide available young women into nice/not-nice categories. 'Tart', 'slag', 'mobby' and 'buffalo girl' are all terms I heard used to describe young women who are considered sexually available or who have already provided themselves as sexual partners for several of the skinheads. Liebow's analysis is especially illuminating when we consider the social significance of this category. He writes (1967, p. 153), 'By claiming to exploit – or actually exploiting – Sally and Irene, Harry is free to declare his liking or love for Mary without seriously compromising his own or others' image of him as the tough and cynical realist'. Following Liebow's reasoning, the category described by 'slag' exists so that skinheads may establish and maintain their subcultural reputations while also fulfilling the responsibilities imposed by a partner. Both Pete and Billy were able to defuse any potential damage to their subcultural reputations by recounting, or having others recount, their sexual exploits. Stories about one's exploitation of women serve to balance the difficulties of retaining a claimed skinhead identity, with all that this entails, with the demands of having a regular partner which may endanger such an identity. In one sense, then, young women are viewed as threatening the brotherhood of skinhead consociation.

Perth skinheads have no explicit label to describe the category of 'nice girl'. For the skinhead set I moved with, this category comprised a core of eight young women which remained remarkably stable despite the influx of assorted other females onto the skinhead scene (and their later departure). Relationships with these young women tended to be of longer duration, perhaps several months, and were based at least partly on feelings of mutual affection. The exploitative aspects were not entirely absent with Roy ending his relationship with one of these young women because he deemed her to be 'a starfish in bed' (not particularly active in sexual play). However, as I described earlier, the behaviours associated with the maintenance and conclusion of some of these relationships suggest that there is considerable emotional investment.

The frequency and nature of a skinhead's casual sexual encounters and the manner of their public representation contribute to subcultural notions about what it is to be a skinhead and what one needs to do to be recognized as a skinhead by other skinheads. Although fighting is paramount and drinking more common, sexual adventures have their place in the construction of legends. Although there is little reward in the skinhead scheme for those entering and maintaining stable relationships with young women, long-term relationships do occur. They contribute more to one's personal identity, as a lover and partner, and sometimes contradict the public subcultural representation.

The position of women

Sue joined the quasi-group originally through being Scouse's 'bird'. After splitting up with him, she had a brief affair with George before moving into a relationship with Rhygin. After a short time Rhygin realized he no longer wished to see her. Because her relationship with Rhygin was obviously fizzling out, Sue slept with Colin. This did not worry Rhygin unduly as he was, for all intents and purposes, 'finished with her anyway'. Following this liaison, Sue had sex with several other skinheads in the space of a few weeks. Although she was not accorded the 'slag' title (she was generally described as a 'bush pig'), she became subject to the most incredible derision and abuse from both skinheads and other young women. Over a period of months she slowly drifted out of the scene. Why was Sue treated so viciously and finally ostracized when other young women, judged to be guilty of similar actions, were not? The answer to this question raises many issues about the place of young women in the skinhead and English scene and about the way in which persons establish their own position in a scene where the rules are notoriously hazy.

I should begin by detailing (from the point of view of the males) more about the numbers, types and positions of the young women who regularly or occasionally mixed with the skinheads with whom I moved. There are eight who form a core – Rachel, Jane, Carol, Sandie, Karen, Michelle, Jessie and the luckless Sue, as well as a number of other young women who periodically enter this circle as the partners of skinheads. In the case of the latter, they usually leave the immediate skinhead scene when the relationship finishes. However, they remain in the broader English scene, often striking up relationships with other members of this scene (such as mods). In addition, several young women also intermittently accompany the core eight but not as partners of the skinheads. They are sisters or friends of the eight. There are also several other young women whom I saw but never met who moved regularly with other sets of skinheads. Whether or not one can describe any of these young women as 'skinheads' or 'skin girls' is a moot point and there is no explicit term for them.[3] They vary greatly in their dress and demeanour. Some wear a version of skinhead uniform; others conform to either more mainstream female fashion or wear the female style common to the English scene, that is, predominantly black in colour with borrowings from the 1960s, 1970s, and 1980s. What unites them is not so much their own style but that of the males and their relationship to them – as sisters, partners, and friends of sisters or partners. For the time of my fieldwork at least, it makes little sense to describe these young women as skinheads. More accurately, they are young women who choose to spend much of their leisure time with skinheads.

I asked Rhygin to categorize the young women in his skinhead circle. True to skinhead culture, he gave me content in the form of identity and biography. For Rhygin, and I had suspected this from my own observation of the interaction between males and females, Rachel, Jane and Carol have special status. They are young women who, through a combination of consociate experience, strength of character and biographical event, have succeeded in becoming honorary men. They have created their own positions which will disappear along with their departure from the skinhead scene. All three have considerable experience of the scene (being in the upper age brackets for females, around eighteen-years-old), all three have been witnessed fighting, none is content with a stereotyped female role. In leisure time, they spend as much time standing with male sets as with other females. As Rhygin puts it, 'They can take the shit the lads give them and give it back'. By contrast, Sandie, Karen, Jessie and Michelle spend more of their time in the company of other females albeit at the same venue as the lads.[4] In addition, he defined a number of young women to be 'bush-pigs'. Broadly speaking, Rhygin has enunciated three categories of young women: those with and those without special status (both categories consisting of potential 'girlfriends'), and those defined as 'slags' or 'bush-pigs'. The latter two categories – potential regular partners without special status and those described as 'slags' – also apply to young women outside skinhead sets. The first, that of special status, does not because detailed biographical knowledge and a history of consociation are required prior to the conferment of such a status. Obviously, these requirements cannot be met by those young women who choose not to participate in skinhead activity.

According to Rhygin (and Rachel), Sue warrants her own category not merely because of her sexual activity, but because of her personality style. According to the other seven young women, Sue is a 'snob', someone who thinks herself better than those surrounding her. Worse still, in the eyes of Rhygin and Rachel, she has no grounds for holding such a self-conception. Sue also lacks close consociate or kinship ties with any of the other young women or the skinheads. Her only link is to Rachel and even this is a tenuous one which became increasingly problematic as time passed. When the abuse began she had no one to turn to for support. I remember being somewhat surprised that she took so long to get the message or, if she had got it, why she persevered. (In one way this shows her strength of character but she could not convert this into behaviour that counted.) Why Sue did not seek to establish ties with Sandie, Karen, Michelle, Jessie, Carol or Jane, nor consolidate her tie with Rachel, I cannot say. One possible explanation for her ostracism is that the young women judged her in terms of their own ideal moral code which disapproved of 'sleeping around' outside the context of a steady relationship (cf. Wilson 1978, Campbell 1984). The young women shun her because her actions and sexual availability make it that much harder for them to maintain their position of sexual restriction in the face of sexual demands from the lads.

In the skinhead context, then, females are generally structurally subordinate and marginal. Exceptions occur where females may create and maintain special positions. The opportunity for females to claim skinhead status is restricted in two ways. First, fighting is the paramount focal concern and means for expression of subcultural attributes and loyalty. It is the essence of legend-making. Skinheads regard females as physically weak and their fights, while they may be discussed (and evaluated and represented as proof of special status), are not the stuff of legends. The second restriction is that female fighting contributes to one's personal identity rather than to a subcultural one, as in the fight between Jane and Pamela described in Chapter Four. There is no archetypal 'skinhead girl' to complement the ideal loyal, hard skinhead male. Campbell (1981) notes this trend in her study of 'delinquent girls': female fights are about slights to personal integrity whereas male fights are also about group honour and loyalty. Rarely does female fighting escalate into a group affair; it remains at the personal level. Therefore, Rachel, Jane and Carol can never become subcultural legends, at least not in male discussions. Instead, their reputations are personal ones based on knowledge of specific biographical events.

For casual sex, skinheads look to a larger universe of females in the English scene. These young women are not unfamiliar with skinheads and, at different times, also form casual and long-term relationships with mods, rockabillies, and other members of the English scene. Regular partners, however, are usually drawn from the eight young women mentioned earlier or from friends of the eight. (I include Sue in the eight as she formed relationships with Scouse and Rhygin prior to her fall from grace.) An informal system operates whereby references are obtained from sisters, brothers, and friends. Sometimes messages are sent first to gauge whether the feelings of a potential partner match those of the message's author. Skinheads may go outside the immediate skinhead scene for sex or try to bring young women into this scene. However, the eight young women identified earlier do not go outside the skinhead scene for male partners; they are drawn exclusively from the skinhead scene. Therefore, skinheads exert a certain control over the partners of 'their' young women – a system of semi-chaperonage. While other skinheads are free to try their luck, outsiders are not. An example will illustrate what may happen if an outsider attempts to gain access to these women.

On walking down an inner-city street en route to a nightclub, Sandie and Karen had been accosted by several young Australian men. Allegedly, one of these men pretended to expose his genitals and made several offensive comments regarding oral sex. Karen, never one to back down from an argument, began arguing with the man. While they were doing so, Billy, Steve, and three other skinheads strolled into view, followed moments later by Rhygin, Les and myself. The odds were now eight of us to four of them. The alleged exposer now began to try to extricate himself from a situation he no longer found to his liking, denying Karen's charge that he had 'flashed' at her. Billy called to Rhygin, indicating that he was to be ready in case of a physical confrontation. Rhygin took up a position close to Billy. The other skinheads arranged themselves in a rough semi-circle around Karen, Billy and the Australians.

At this point, an English man in his late twenties arrived on the scene, an ex-skinhead named Charlie who knew Billy. Billy explained the situation to Charlie, who had moved through the small crowd to stand beside him. Charlie then assumed responsibility for

Karen's argument and the tone of the altercation became more aggressive. The Australian man also sensed this change and his efforts to placate Charlie became more desperate. Charlie then head-butted the Australian in the face, knocking him to the footpath. His shaken response was, 'She's right, mate! She's right!' As he rose slowly from the ground, Charlie grabbed his shirt and pushed him roughly towards his friends, who now appeared quite anxious. Billy then intervened and threatened, 'Scrap or run!' The Australian set left hurriedly.

The sentimental model

For skinheads there are subcultural notions as to appropriate behaviour towards women. With respect to the young women who associate with skinheads, the situation is rather different. There is little in the way of a subcultural mode to guide behaviour. Female ideas belong to a more personal mode. They appear to be based on a notion of love which corresponds with what Hannerz (1969) calls the 'sentimental model' (and what McRobbie [1978] terms the 'culture of femininity'). Hannerz discusses the 'sentimental model' of the American mainstream family, that is, the man as head of the household and breadwinner and the wife as mother and homemaker. The ghetto African Americans he studied are exposed to these norms via such cultural apparatus as radio, television, and newspapers. The model transmitted may bear some relation to reality but is a sentimental model which people try to live up to. The young women with whom skinheads associate are not trying to live up to a sentimental model of marriage; theirs is one of courtship, young love, and romance.

For methodological reasons (see Note 1), my data on this subject are limited but I was privy to two interesting conversations which occurred only moments apart involving Jane, Michelle, two skinheads, and myself. The two young women were abusing one of the skinheads over his liaison with another young woman which resulted in pregnancy. The criticism centred around the skinhead's lack of true feeling for the young woman – she had been a 'one-night stand'. Both young women objected to the notion of casual sex. The targeted skinhead replied aggressively to Michelle, 'Why did you fuck Roy?' Michelle's reply: 'Because I loved him! ... Then'.

Minutes later, the same five were discussing an interview they had seen on television with an outspoken female representative from the Rajneeshi religious sect. (There had been some controversy over their plan to convert a town in the southwest of Western

alia into a commune. The various current affairs television
ammes and the local newspapers had run several interviews.)
rently, as Jane and Michelle told it, the spokeswoman had
used the movement's philosophy as one of free love and sex
staring that she personally had seven lovers and permitted her
young daughter to watch her engaging in sex. Whatever the
accuracy of their account, Jane and Michelle highlighted the sexual
aspects of the interview they had seen. They were objecting to
notions of casual sex or at least sex outside the traditional
'boyfriend'/'girlfriend' relationship. While the young women made
no claims to their own innocence, they were pointing to their
attempted adherence to a code which forbade sex outside a
relationship based on intimacy and emotional investment.

These examples relate to the mainstream sentimental model.[5]
There are also uglier aspects to this model such as Karen's
admission to Rhygin that she had ended their relationship because
he did not 'keep her in line', through physical force if necessary. The
point is that the 'nice skinhead girls' appear to hold a view of
relationships which is based on intimate feelings for their partner.
Only within this context is a sexual relationship acceptable. Young
women do not hold an exploitative view of men, at least not overtly.
Perhaps this is the key to understanding Sue's position of ridicule.
She took on a role allocated to men, as exploiter of the opposite sex,
and therefore provided a disquieting challenge that was met with
ostracism by both women and men.[6]

A constant theme which runs through skinhead relationships with
young women is the difference between the subcultural consequences of one's actions, that is, the consequences for one's
reputation as a skinhead in the eyes of other skinheads, and the
consequences for one's personal identity. Stories and public representations as 'seeker of sex' provide evidence to support one's claim
to be a skinhead. However, observation of actual incidents demonstrates that this categorical representation is mediated by
situational, personal, and emotional factors. These two levels, the
subcultural and the personal, are germane to the understanding of
the larger category of male representations of which stories about
sexual exploits are just one part, that of 'memories'. 'Memories' and
how one goes about gaining them is my concern in the next chapter.

Notes

1. Feminist writers on youth (e.g., Campbell 1984, McRobbie 1980, McRobbie and Garber 1976) have rightly criticized the mostly male authors of existing sociological accounts of youth subcultures for failing to account for females in their studies. They have also noted that when females are included in accounts they are generally discussed through the perspective of males, a criticism which could be made of my research. One possible answer to this criticism for those who choose participant observation as their principal research method is provided by Hannerz (1969, p. 209), writing of his fieldwork experience amongst African Americans in Washington. He states that because the 'ghetto community' he studied was divided along sex lines, he was much more able to establish close friendships with men, and to participate in their activities, than he was with women. Many of the women he got to know better were, in some way, closely connected to the men he knew – 'they were their wives, girl friends, sisters, daughters, and so forth' – and were fairly marginal to the activities of those he counted amongst his 'closer circle'. To intensify contacts with women would have raised suspicions amongst the men who viewed male/female relationships primarily in sexual terms. Substitute 'skinhead subculture' for 'ghetto community' and my problems in collecting data on females match those of Hannerz. Like the skinheads, I was not privy to all-female conversations, an inability born of the field, and my understanding and discussion of the relationships between skinheads and young women is necessarily presented from the point of view of the males with whom I moved.

2. Exploitation for material gain is not usually a motivation because the young women with whom skinheads generally interact are not often in particularly advantageous financial positions – being young and sometimes unemployed. Besides, money is not a particularly valued commodity.

3. In England, young skinhead women were sometimes known as 'rennes' (Knight 1982, p. 20).

4. In spending time together, Sandie, Karen, Jessie and Michelle no doubt created their own set of understandings about men/women relationships to which a male researcher was not privy (see Note 1).

5. See Frith (1981) for an examination of similar issues in popular music.

6. It is worth noting that Rhygin disagreed with this interpretation. His disagreement raises the question of ethnographic authority which is discussed in several of the essays in Clifford and Marcus (1986).

8 'Memories' and the creation of identity

'They were the three best nights I think we've had' was a comment made by Rhygin about what I have called the 'Ipswich Nights'. These nights, even though they occurred in 1983, were fervently discussed throughout my fieldwork with particular reference to the parts played by the skinheads present. This chapter is about the represent-ation of such past events in stories, a process which leads to the creation and consolidation of 'memories' and to the attribution of id-entity. I discuss stories of two sorts: those told to me during informal interviews, and those heard in everyday skinhead conversation.

The analysis of memories and their significance for skinheads is vital. Memories relate closely to skinhead ideas of identity and value and so are part of what 'being a skinhead' is all about. Inquiries about the research from skinheads usually took the form, 'Did you write down what happened last night?' meaning had I recorded actual events. When I answered in the affirmative they approved because I was making their exploits and adventures tangible and preserved. Their 'memories' had been recorded. For anthropology in general, the discussion adds to the study of social collectivities whose members base their social ranking and evaluation of persons on past and present events, that is, people who subscribe to the principle that one is what one does or has done. This principle corresponds with Sansom's 'consociate identity'. For skinheads, consociate identity is 'accorded or is claimed with reference to a person's history of co-participation with others in happenings' (Sansom 1980, p. 139). Per-sonal history is mapped via events, shifts in venue and scene, changes in style, and alterations in relationships to quasi-groups and the derived action-sets.

Consociate identity is derived from the aggregation of memories which fall into two categories, 'the good night' and 'the good laugh'. These categories pertain to different action and result in different ng of a person's identity. The 'good night' label is applied to events which yield social prestige for the skinheads involved in . By social prestige, I mean that the skinheads who participate he good night have enhanced their reputations as 'skinheads' among consociates. The status accorded to the skinhead for his actions is expressed in such ways as 'He's the hardest fuckin' bastard in this pub' or 'He really pulls the birds'. The positive judgement in these evaluations is of the young man's performance as a skinhead. He must fulfil certain requirements to be a skinhead, the most important of which is fighting and being loyal to friends in violent situations. To a lesser extent, drinking and womanizing are also valued. It is from such stuff that skinhead legends are made.

By contrast, the 'good laugh' labels those events which fall outside the 'good night' category. The 'good laugh' states less about the person's performance as a skinhead, more about the young man as a person. Whereas the 'good night' belongs to the skinhead subculture, to be told and retold in the manufacturing of skinhead reputation, the 'good laugh' helps to mark the close relationships between friends and amongst members of the action-set. Events labelled as 'good laughs' do not usually add to one's reputation as a skinhead and therefore do not have significance at the broad subcultural level. However, these events flesh out a skinhead to give him a personality among his intimates.

The distinction between the good night and the good laugh is central to this chapter. Good nights are symbolic events which celebrate skinhead unity and solidarity through collectively being 'out with the lads'. Through participation in such nights, skinheads reaffirm their personal belief in the validity of these occasions and their categorical identities as 'skinheads'. The good laugh has no such symbolic dimension. To clarify the distinction between the social consequences of the good night and the good laugh, I will call additions to a person's reputation as a skinhead (which derives from participation in good nights), additions to 'subcultural' or 'categorical identity'. The additions of a more personal nature amongst friends (derived from incidents described as 'good laughs') are additions to 'personal identity'. Taken together, these two concepts make up Sansom's 'consociate identity'. Whenever I discuss identity or reputation as 'subcultural' or 'personal', I refer to the level to which these attributions belong. Some events have significance for both legend-making and personal identity.

The good night

One unit of experience that has a rare and explicit label in the sparse skinhead argot is the 'good night'. Skinheads define its ideal constituents as 'Getting pissed, pulling a bird and having a fight'. For a skinhead, a night containing all three would indeed be good. The good night always centres around heavy drinking and those activities usually associated with the heavy drinking context – specifically interpersonal violence between skinheads and members of other youth subcultures and, less often, casual sexual encounters with women. Fighting and drinking will suffice if eligible females are unavailable or an attempt to 'pull' a young woman is unsuccessful. More often, a night considered 'boring' can be transformed by a single incident into a memorable evening. Good nights usually occur in mixed venues or in occasional venues rather than in regular venues (where skinheads usually keep the peace and so eliminate one avenue of excitement). They belong to places where the potential for fighting is greatest. In the mixed or occasional venue, skinheads are more likely to encounter hostile elements of other youth subcultures. The opposition is often unknown in terms of past participation in scenes and eras and therefore questions of network links and choosing sides are made irrelevant.

About a year before my fieldwork began, the skinheads I was later to know were involved in a series of incidents which, as I noted above, Rhygin declared to be 'the three best nights I think we've had'. In reporting them, I have relied on Rhygin's diary account supplemented by a lengthy taped interview, thus highlighting his perceptions of the evenings. As a cross-check, I have also noted the reconstructions of the evenings by others. In addition, much of the type of action described in the following account of these incidents also occurred in many other instances. Despite my absence from these particular evenings, I can testify to their consistency with skinhead modes of thought and behaviour. What follows, then, is a description of what I have christened 'the Ipswich Nights'.

Rhygin had been associating with Mick and Joe and some other skinheads from Perth's northern suburbs. On the first of what became three consecutive Saturday nights, Rhygin and several skinheads and young women drove to an hotel to the south of Perth, The Ipswich, to see a ska band.[1] On entering the pub they found it crowded with moidies. Rhygin remarked that the moidies looked as though 'they'd come straight from work', a comment on what he perceived to be a lack of style on the part of the Australian male. (It is, in fact, just a different style disapproved of by the stylistic chauvinism of skinheads.) As they moved further into the pub, Rhygin and his associates spied another set of skinheads sitting at a table. After buying drinks Rhygin's set got talking to the other skinheads, finding out names, addresses and birthplaces in England, and where they lived in Perth. (They were from several of Perth's southern suburbs.) The band began playing and several males from both sets began dancing together in the all-male skinhead style. They also continued to drink until they were 'rotten pissed'. The boisterous skinhead dancing style usually involves at least several skinheads in a rough circle, dancing vigorously on the spot, kicking boots up into the middle of the circle, or rhythmically jumping and kicking from side to side. The emphasis is often on creating as much mayhem as possible. In this way, dancing expresses group solidarity.

Then the trouble began. An 'Aussie' at the bar had been 'taking the piss' by dancing in an exaggerated version of the skinheads' movements. He was also staring at Smithy, one of the southern skinheads, and beckoning him to come and fight. Eventually the man came striding to the table. Smithy stood up and the two began swinging fists. They moved onto the dance floor still fighting. As neither seemed to be winning the other skinheads stood by and watched, which in itself was unusual. Then four Aussies, presumably mates of Smithy's opponent, came running towards the two protagonists. Rhygin and a couple of other skinheads moved to block their path, Rhygin throwing a glass. The would-be rescuers turned tail and retreated.

Joe tackled the original assailant and tripped him to the floor. Both fell together and Joe started kicking the Aussie in the upper body. Mick also joined in and began jumping on the opponent's head. Joe and Mick then stopped, expecting to see a horde of other Aussies surrounding them. This did not happen. Instead, the assembled audience stood watching. Then the barman and another man came over, lifted the prone Aussie to his feet and helped him away. Mick and Joe each kept one of the man's thongs, one of his signs of Australian identity, as 'trophies' of their victory over what they saw to be a symbol of Australia.

This fight formed a bond between the two sets of skinheads because of the willingness of Rhygin and his set to act in Smithy's defence. The two sets agreed to meet at the same pub the following Saturday. For the next two Saturdays they did meet and both occasions qualified as 'good nights'. There was more fighting, more drinking and more camaraderie as the skinheads got to know one another better. These nights are still talked about fervently and in great detail. Most of the conversation centres on the participation of persons in the events. For example, whenever someone mentions the incident which involved throwing a glass at the opponents, Scouse inevitably pipes up with 'And you nearly hit me with it, an' all!' The purpose of these sessions is to allow each skinhead the chance to make clear that he was present on this good night and to claim a stake in the glory attached to it.

Other celebrated occasions are usually less dramatic with a single spectacular event being sufficient to transform an otherwise mediocre night into one considered 'good'. Rhygin, several other skinheads and I had spent the evening at Darcy's and following this arranged to continue drinking at a nightclub. Of the regular set, Rhygin, Ace, Sue, Chris, Jane and I were present at the nightclub. After about an hour, Rhygin and I found ourselves sitting with Jim and Lisa. Jim said that several men sitting to Rhygin's rear were 'eyeing us up'. (Jim later stated that one of them had thrown a lighted cigarette butt at Rhygin.) Jim reckoned we should 'have them' and asked me, 'Are you in?' I replied, implying a bravery I did not feel, 'Only if Rhygin gets into trouble'. This satisfied Jim who expressed no surprise at my 'only-if-Rhygin's-in-trouble' answer. Rhygin said he was 'in' and handed his expensive and hard to obtain Fred Perry cardigan to Lisa.

Jim called to one of the other set, 'When I finish this drink I'm going to come over there and rip your face off!' He then continued to stare belligerently at the other set, his intentions unmistakable. Jim took a final swig from his beer bottle and passed it to Rhygin who emptied it and then turned, hurling the bottle at the other set. Both skinheads then stormed over and began fighting with the others. Jim grabbed one and managed to get a few punches in before three bouncers appeared. For some reason the bouncers had singled out Jim for special attention, rather than Rhygin, and they began dragging him forcibly to the exit. Rhygin followed untouched. While being removed from the premises Jim repeatedly yelled to his opponent to 'come outside'. Once on the street it transpired that Rhygin's bottle had hit a female member of the other set in the head. She emerged with her friends. On seeing them, Jim again challenged his opponent to fight.

Then another man who had not been a part of the original fracas in the club walked up to Jim. He was presumably a friend of the non-skinheads. He walked to a large window-sill that jutted from the front of the hotel, methodically removed his glasses, jumper and shirt, and stood, bare-chested, accusing Jim of being the launcher of the thrown bottle and challenging him to fight. Jim denied guilt and his denial was true as Rhygin had been the culprit. The bare-chested man continued his accusations while Jim denied them. The two progressed down the street, Jim walking backwards under the verbal onslaught. Rhygin stayed near Jim. The Australian repeatedly challenged Jim to fight him instead of 'throwing bottles at girls' but Jim would not be goaded. The two skinheads had backed up the street about forty yards before the aggressor gave up in disgust and returned to his possessions on the window-sill. After the incident, as we walked to my car, Jim gave a clenched fist salute and yelled, 'The lads!' and 'The lads in action!' Later, after I had granted Jim his request for a lift to another nightclub, Jim thanked Rhygin for the fight.

On another occasion, late one Friday evening, Ace, Rhygin and I were walking through Northbridge, an area of inner-city Perth popular for its nightclubs, restaurants, brothels, and illegal gambling houses. After speaking on the street to several people that either Rhygin or Ace knew, we began walking back to my car having decided that for us the night was over. A green Toyota drove past and Ace exclaimed, 'That was Carson with six mates! Quick, he's going round the park!' (Carson is a bog well known to Ace.) Rhygin and I thought Ace was joking or mistaken as he has proven to be on other such occasions. Moments later, the Toyota swung around the corner with Carson and a friend of his, Ken, inside. The Toyota stopped in the middle of the street and to my surprise Ace and Rhygin went over and began chatting at the driver's open window. I stayed on the kerb and was later told about the conversation which I could see was becoming more and more heated as it progressed. Carson was telling Ace he would fight Nutter 'one-to-one, any time, anywhere!'[2] Ace responded with the threat that should any harm come to Nutter, he and several other skinheads would wreak havoc with Carson's family home. This incensed Carson. Ken, who had not spoken until now, turned to me and calmly said, 'Take your mate away'. I replied, 'It's his argument. It's nothing to do with me'. At this point Carson removed his seat-belt. Seconds later, Ace punched Carson in the face and kicked the car door. Rhygin also managed to punch Carson in the face. Carson recovered surprisingly quickly, leapt out of the car and chased Rhygin towards a nearby park. Ace raced around to the front of the car near me as Ken climbed out of the passenger seat waving a pair of nunchukas – a martial arts weapon consisting of two short, cylindrical pieces of hardened wood joined by a chain. Seeing this, Ace yelled, 'Run, Dave!' and we both wasted no time. Ken half-heartedly gave chase, stopping after fifteen yards or so, while we pelted down the road to the comparative safety of some railway lines. Here Ace lifted a piece of metal pipe and screamed back up the street, 'Come on then, Ken, I'll 'ave you!' I said, 'Put the pipe down and let's get to the car'. Driving around we spotted an exhausted-looking Rhygin, picked him up and headed for home. Later in the week, Rhygin and Ace learnt that during the scuffle they had inflicted a black eye on Carson and dented his car door. Both derived considerable pleasure from this news and were also accorded credit by those other skinheads of the quasi-group who disliked Carson.

One incident that became the subject of an oft-repeated story was Rhygin's head-butt of a mod opponent during an altercation at a nightclub. Despite there being no clear-cut winner of the fight, Ace thought it 'the best fuckin' head-butt I've ever seen!' This supreme evaluation, by someone who had witnessed the original incident (and been involved in the ensuing violence), reinforced Rhygin's reputation as a good fighter by according a high level of competence to him in a subculturally valued activity. Other skinheads, on hearing Ace's glowing report and seeing his mimed recreation of the event, echoed Ace's verdict.

In these events the common feature was an uneventful evening suddenly transformed by the irruptive incidents described. These incidents were sufficient to mark each night 'good'. The skinheads concerned had been involved in violence and, although not winning convincingly, had emerged from the action unhurt and after inflicting some injury on the opposition. They had proved their willingness both to fight and to aid each other in dangerous situations of their own making. Consequently, their reputations as skinheads had been enhanced by their participation in the incidents.

On another evening, the sexual aspects of which I described in Chapter Seven, Nutter, Rhygin, Billy, Ace, Sue and Rachel had met in Darcy's and then moved on to a nightclub. A young woman called Kate and two of her female friends also turned up. Rhygin described the evening as enjoyable because time had not dragged by, with everyone dancing, drinking, and generally 'having a good laugh'. Both Rhygin and Billy 'had a go' at different men during the course of the evening but nothing came of it. Later, Billy began talking to Kate as she had been deserted by her two friends. Ace, Rhygin, Nutter, Rachel and Sue now decided that they'd had enough and were organizing to leave. They asked Billy, who was talking to Kate, if he was coming with them. He replied that he would be 'out in a minute'. As things turned out, Billy did not leave with the other skinheads but spent the night with Kate. He arrived back at Ace's early Sunday morning.

I arrived at Ace's about lunchtime on the Sunday in time to hear the lengthy dissection of the previous evening's activities. The public pronouncement of Billy, the skinhead central to the stories, was that it had been a 'good night' because he had a 'bit of aggro, pulled a bird, and got pissed'. The other skinheads present agreed whole-heartedly with his analysis. Almost every incident was discussed from the vantage point of each person present. The stories of the evening's activities served collectively to reinforce skinhead values through the positive evaluation of experience, and to enhance Billy's reputation as a person of considerable note in the subculture.

Importantly, there is also an element of vicarious experience present in these discussions. Only one skinhead fulfilled the three requirements for a good night, yet all those present on the evening also claimed it was such a night. They discussed their own roles in the evening's events as well as that of Billy. The vicarious process works in the following way. Billy had a good night. Consequently, he drew admiration from the others which added to his subcultural reputation as being an effective 'puller of birds', fighter and drinker. It was another entry in his logbook of subcultural fame. The others present have a vested interest in establishing their participation in what has been defined as a prized event. Not every skinhead has the personal characteristics – such attributes as confidence, fighting ability and wit – to become a well-known identity. But those who fall short of this mark can soften the blow by resorting to glory-by-association. Talking about an event is enhanced if all present on the original evening agree about its quality. There is collective reinforce-ment of one another. Embellishment of the events, and of persons' participation in them, serves in retrospect to make the good night more memorable than it actually was. It serves to make the good night and skinhead leisure style worthwhile.

The good laugh

'Good laughs' are those instances which make no addition to a person's subcultural reputation as a 'skinhead' but which are remembered by the action-set involved. Good laughs concern humorous situations which may arise as an unintended consequence of other action, as was the case in the following incident. On several occasions skinheads organized thefts from bottleshops. One person would buy an item and thus occupy the proprietor at the cash register while the others shoplifted. The aim was to steal enough alcohol to get 'pissed' without paying. After one successful raid, the spoils were counted with the best 'buy' being a bottle of whisky. Pete revealed his acquired commodity – a bottle of non-alcoholic spirits marketed under the name 'Claytons'. (Clayton's is a beverage made well known in Australia through an extensive television advertising campaign which has spawned a number of 'Clayton's jokes'. These jokes have guaranteed the term 'Clayton's' currency in the popular idiom as a word for a substitute or sham.) Pete was the butt of immediate derision from the others. Whenever the subject of stealing from bottleshops is discussed this incident is inevitably mentioned if any of the original set are present. These insults were not intended to be harmful however. The incident is viewed as a demonstration of Pete's personality. The story caused little surprise when recounted to others not present at the original incident but familiar with Pete. In a similar raid on a bottleshop several weeks later, Pete stole a bottle of bitters. This again brought scorn and ridicule from other skinheads until someone read the label and discovered the high alcohol content. It was then consumed with Coca-Cola. Despite the bitters turning out to be alcoholic and thus a successful theft, the fact that it was bitters rather than some more conventional alcoholic drink (say, whisky or vodka) again reflected on Pete. The end result was an addition to, or confirmation of, his personal identity amongst friends.

Although difficult to label, Pete's identity was established as someone who did not always think sufficiently before acting; of someone who was gullible and not always quick to grasp a joke. During one evening at Darcy's, a skinhead put a riddle to the set he was standing with, 'What's the difference between a camel and a suckworth?' Inevitably, someone asked, 'What's a suckworth?' and the crude pun was recognized. However, Pete still did not get it. He asked what a 'suckworth' was and it was left to a patient Rhygin and Nutter to explain the humour to Pete. The point is this: Pete's identity did not require an explicit label because those who knew him well enough to pass judgement would be familiar with such incidents as the Clayton's theft. Pete's personality was not something that would interest all skinheads, only those comprising his current action-set. The response of friends when hearing of Pete's escapades was, 'That's just like Pete'.

Another example of how personal identity may be created by a good laugh occurred one Saturday night. Word of a party at 'the Uni' had reached some of the skinheads and they decided to gate-crash. We drove to the university – Rhygin, Terry, Jack and Nutter in my car, Ace, Rachel and Roy in Roy's car – but could see no evidence of any party. Some students were sighted so we drove past in order to ask them if they knew about the party. As Terry was closest to the window he volunteered and asked, in an exaggerated Australian accent, 'Hey moidies, do ya know where the pardy is?' This brought gales of laughter from the other occupants of my car who were not expecting this impersonation and who appreciated the 'taking-the-piss' aspect of the humour. This incident is also referred to often and comments on Terry's accepted wit and reputation amongst his friends. This again adds up to a statement similar to that identifying Ace, 'You know what Terry's like'.

Other good laughs may be long-term affairs such as a competition known as 'the bet' which ran sporadically for several months. The aim, established on the first night, was to 'pick up a bird who was better than a bush pig' and who was previously unknown to the participants. The standard of 'bush pig' was set at 'uglier' than one of the females known to the participants in the competition. To win, all one had to do was 'get off with' (defined for the purposes of the bet as 'kissing') the target in view of the others and this would win one a pint of beer from each of the witnesses. It was also tacitly agreed that if one was near success the others could spoil one's ploy by interrupting. Eyes were cast over available females and much daring and evaluating done. On one occasion I was innocently speaking to a young woman I had met through another acquaintance. As the music was very loud I turned and spoke into her ear. From his vantage point, Ace thought I was kissing her and came rushing over. He bluntly asked me, 'Have you won the bet?' The young woman looked perplexed, I felt embarrassed, and the others just laughed. In this particular case, I was the subject of the good laugh.

However, not all good laughs have such harmless beginnings. One story I heard concerned a set of skinheads who, bored with the night's proceedings at a pub, decided to visit a car park known to be a meeting place for bogs. The set went down 'for a laugh' but turned tail on sighting vast numbers of bogs who gave chase through Perth. The skinheads escaped and the incident was described as a 'good laugh'. Nothing had been achieved in terms of additions to reputation – the skinheads had fled – but for the action-set involved it contained excitement, the threat of physical injury, and the element of 'it's funny when you look back on it'.

Good laughs can also be created at someone else's expense, as the result of a practical joke. Rhygin, Rachel and Nutter were walking through Perth's central pedestrian shopping mall one lunchtime. They overtook an elderly gentleman walking in the same direction and wearing a hat. As she passed him, Rachel knocked the hat from his head. Rhygin had walked on the other side of the old man. The old man, assuming Rhygin to be the culprit, turned and punched him in the stomach. He then stormed off cursing the skinheads. Nutter and Rachel were in hysterics by now at their framing of the innocent Rhygin who, while unhurt, was utterly bewildered by the old man's actions. Nutter and Rachel decided Rhygin had been 'beaten up by a sixty-five-year-old man' and were quick to pass the information to others who knew Rhygin but were not present. The contrast of the hardened skinhead being 'beaten up' by this elderly man provided the basis for much subsequent stirring of Rhygin for several days and was mentioned occasionally for several months.

There is also a sub-category of the 'good laugh'. Some incidents, while having primary importance for the action-set, may also have modest repercussions for a skinhead's reputation in the subculture. Minor infractions of the law add to one's general reputation in terms of the flouting of authority but not specifically to a person's skinhead identity. For example, skinheads sometimes 'jump' a taxi home. This practice involves catching a taxi, usually from central Perth, in the early hours of the morning and on arriving near home, exiting the taxi without paying. The skinheads I moved with jumped taxis on several occasions, being looked upon as a regular way home if there were no lifts available. While jumping a taxi adds no skinhead worth it does establish the jumpers as devil-may-care.

A specific example of an event which yielded subcultural kudos but the importance of which lay primarily with the action-set is provided by an incident in an inner-city pub. Rhygin, Ace, Paul and I were sitting at a table in the pub's lounge. Three females, including Carol, Paul's girlfriend, were talking to a set of males at the bar in an effort to obtain free drinks. The young women then sat down at the table next to ours. One of the men at the bar walked across the room, knelt by their table and said something to Carol before leaving to rejoin his friends. Apparently, the man, who appeared quite drunk, had asked for certain sexual favours in return for the free drinks. Carol told Rhygin what the man had said, requesting that he not tell Paul and thereby risk 'trouble'. (Carol apparently thought that Paul, as her boyfriend, might want to take the matter up with the man.) Rhygin, spoiling for some excitement, immediately told Paul. Paul said he would rather not fight because we were outnumbered. Rhygin immediately stood up and began counting the set of strangers at the bar in a very obvious and exaggerated manner. One of the set witnessed Rhygin's actions and arrived at our table belligerent and drunk. He asked Rhygin what he had been doing. Rhygin replied truthfully, 'I was counting you'. The antagonist dismissed us with a drunken comment and returned to his set. We decided to leave as there were seven of 'them' versus our four. Rhygin, who had been drinking cider, retained his empty 'stubbie' (a 375ml bottle). As we passed the other set Paul dared him to throw it. Rhygin gleefully accepted the dare and sent the stubbie flying into their midst as we ran out of the door of the pub. Seconds later, several unhappy men, recently surprised by the unheralded arrival of an empty cider stubbie, spilled onto the pavement, spied us escaping up the street and gave chase. After about a hundred yards, they gave up and we slowed to a brisk walk. However, our haste had been noticed by two policemen on patrol. We were warned that if there were any reports of trouble in the area 'we'll know where to come looking'.

The major contribution of this incident was to Rhygin's reputation as a 'mad' character for throwing the bottle. During later conversation, it was described as a 'good laugh' and Rhygin explained his reason for throwing the bottle as being 'for a laugh'. Clearly, the primary importance of the event lay with the action-set, with some limited addition to skinhead reputation being gained from contact with the police and from wilfully inviting physical danger. Such memories comment on personal identity above that of the basic 'skinhead'. Usually these activities provide no addition in the subcultural sense, that is, they do little or nothing to enhance reputations or to create skinhead heroes. Their significance lies in the action-set and in their role as partial reward for the investment of time and energy.

The creation of identity

Skinhead activity is about making memories – whether they be of the subcultural or personal variety.[3] Having a fund of stories, or being able to assert that 'I was there when so and so happened', is important as it announces one's subcultural investment of time and energy and therefore one's authenticity.

A good night enhances the reputations of those who participate in it if the performances of any of them are impressive. In conversation, the information flow guarantees that exploits become known. Even after nights where skinheads fare second-best in any violence the effect may still be positive. One skinhead visited Darcy's a week after he had been injured in a fight. At one point during the evening, another skinhead spoke to him, looked at the wound and appreciative 'Not bad'. The injury was concrete evidence skinhead's total involvement in a past event.

Once a skinhead has participated in several good nights been regularly involved in skinhead activity for some time regation of these events bestows the status of known identity. He is recognized in the skinhead subculture and possibly the wider English scene, has an extensive quasi-group from which to draw action-sets, and possesses a considerable store of memories. Being a known identity results from adequate performance in subculturally approved activities, for example, holding one's own in fights or occasionally 'pulling a bird'. Should the skinhead's performance in these activities be more than satisfactory he may be accorded a higher level of competence. For example, if a skinhead wins his fights then he earns the right to be called 'hard'. Fame is assured in the skinhead subculture and possibly in the wider English scene.

Implicit in the development of reputation is the process whereby repeated collective judgement is brought down on a person's actions. The telling and re-telling of stories and the spread of information about deeds throughout the subculture, with inevitable and sometimes intentional distortion, leads to the consolidation of subcultural identity and a place in skinhead lore for those positively evaluated in the stories. The skinheads known to me often spoke of Robbo as 'the hardest' skinhead but knew little of him personally, such knowledge being reserved for those in his action-set. But the stories had circulated and from several oft-repeated tales of his exploits Robbo's reputation was assured. It is in the telling and re-telling of stories that fame is manufactured. Such stories become the social currency of subcultural identity; they yield prestige for the participants. Without an adequate fund of these memories which attest to one's successful involvement in subculturally valued activities, one's reputation cannot flourish but dies a social death.

There is also a tendency for skinheads to remember and embellish the past and to de-emphasize the present. The construction and re-construction of stories only occurs over a lengthy period and events do not become the stuff of good nights and memories for some considerable time. Time must elapse for the less favourable aspects of events to be forgotten or deemed less important and for the positive aspects to be embellished, redefined and rejuvenated. Sometimes good nights will not be perceived as such until the same set of skinheads are together again to discuss the minutiae of the original event. This might not happen for some weeks or even

..onths. Alternatively, the good night may be recognized as such after a relatively short period but it may still require a number of further tellings to become indelibly stamped into skinhead lore.

Returning to consociate identity, the uses of story combine to assert that a skinhead is what he has done and so can lay no claim to entitlement if investment in action is absent. This again relates to ownership of style in that one cannot claim to be what one has not worked to earn. Thus, one skinhead who claimed to be the 'hardest skinhead in town' was denied his self-proclaimed ranking because his prior fighting record proved insufficiently impressive.[4]

In contrast to the good night, the good laugh has a different social import. A skinhead is what he has done not only for his subcultural reputation as a skinhead (is he a good fighter, good drinker, woman-izer?) but also in relation to his current action-set. While his skinhead identity rests largely on good nights, the rounding-out of the skin-head as a person, the additional characteristics and idiosyncrasies that make up any personality, are given vent in closer relationships such as the good laugh. These implicit, and sometimes explicit, attributions about individuality counterbalance the more categorical identity supported by the good night. I spoke to several skinheads who had fearsome reputations but who in conversation appeared far more sedate and sociable than their notoriety would lead one to believe.

The meaning of the good laugh is grounded in more specific relationships between closer friends. It makes little sense to those of sufficient social distance to lack biographical knowledge of those involved in the original event. Whereas the good night belongs to the skinhead subculture, to be told and retold in the manufacturing of skinhead reputation, good laughs help to mark the close relationships between friends and amongst members of the action-set. The good laugh states less about a young man's performance as a skinhead and more about him as a person.

For Perth skinheads, good nights are more significant than good laughs because they are symbolic events which celebrate skinhead unity and solidarity through collectively being 'out with the lads'. Through 'getting pissed, pulling a bird and having a fight', skinheads reaffirm their belief in the validity of these occasions and their categorical identities as skinheads. Being a skinhead is about invest-ing time with other skinheads and the return on this investment is a fund of stories about one's participation in these famous nights. Being part of a good night is a symbolic action which signals the embracing of the skinhead ethos. Good laughs mean a great deal personally but do not go to the heart of skinhead identity; they have no such symbolic dimension. Taken together, memories bring the past into the present which is dominated by current particularities and understandings about a skinhead's subcultural and personal identity. However, it is through participation in good nights that a skinhead really becomes a skinhead.

Notes

1. Ska music originated in Jamaica in the early 1960s and was brought to England by Jamaican rude boys soon afterwards. The musical ancestor of reggae, ska has been described as 'clammy, pelvic and throbbing' and as having a 'nagging, echoing, simple upbeat' (Knight 1982, p. 14). Ska's principal early artists were Desmond Dekker, Laurel Aitken and Prince Buster who were later to inspire English music trends and bands such as Madness and The Selector.

2. Carson, a member of a rival set of bogs, held a long-standing grudge against Nutter over past events.

3. See Burns (1980) for an account of similar processes.

4. Some skinheads also recognized that this title is purely hypothetical as one could not fight everyone to prove the claim.

9 Social process and youth subcultures

So far, this book has been about the exploits of a particular set of young people. This final chapter is one of conclusions in which I present an anthropology of social process, examine the related notions of authenticity and sincerity, and spell out the implications of the study for anthropology and for the notion of multiculturalism in Australia.

The skinhead subculture is labile, that is, one in which the composition of action-sets and quasi-groups, and the relationships between persons within these types of grouping, are subject to frequent change. Skinheads belong to a category of persons, the skinhead subculture, which contains overlapping quasi-groups usually linked by ties between their members. These links have been formed in past consociate eras. From these quasi-groups are drawn action-sets for specific consociate activity on particular social occasions. The action-set is the basic unit of social activity and usually consists of between three and six skinheads. Monitoring several such sets in succession allows identification of the quasi-group from which persons are most often recruited to form future action-sets. Cliques may form if several skinheads are all close consociates of one another and form action-sets frequently. I demonstrated this ongoing process in Chapter Two with an account of Rhygin's switching of quasi-groups and action-sets over a five-year period. Because of Rhygin's long involvement in the skinhead subculture and larger English scene, his network of bridging ties is larger than that of a newcomer to the scene. The process by which action-sets become quasi-groups and quasi-groups lead to the formation of future action-sets is cyclical as future action-sets are drawn from the quasi-group, yet several action-sets need to be formed before the quasi-group can be identified.

In the same way that action-set relates to quasi-group, so venue relates to scene. Scenes are spatio-temporal domains which characterize the day and nightlife of a city. They are established independently of those skinheads who may frequent them. Venues are specific scenes patronized by skinheads in the company of other skinheads at arranged times. Regular venues are seen by skinheads as their scenes. A skinhead action-set will patronize a scene for some time, transforming it into their venue by their presence and thereby transforming the scene. Over a period of time, skinhead patronage will switch to other scenes, transforming the old venue back into a scene and transforming the new scene into a venue by virtue of their physical presence. Venue and scene co-exist with the physical presence of skinheads transforming a scene into their venue. At any one time, there are several skinhead scenes, one of which a skinhead action-set will choose on a specific occasion and thus transform it into their venue.

The choosing of a scene, which then becomes a venue, may result in activity described as 'good nights' or 'good laughs'. The subsequent events become the subject of specific 'memories' and are remembered fondly. Should several good nights be had at a particular venue then this period of attendance may become an era, one to be especially remembered as a time marked by distinctive acts and flavour. Memories celebrate the activities of the action-set and contribute to the recognition of a worthwhile quasi-group. In the process of the telling and re-telling of such stories, skinheads validate the existence of a quasi-group which was, and is, successful in the search for good times. A skinhead action-set may have venues for different days or nights of the week and, consequently, the era evoked in stories may encompass several venues.

Many social contacts are developed during one's career in the English scene and sociable interaction with members of other youth subcultures is not unusual (see Chapter Five). A young man may move through a succession of subcultures – skinhead, mod, teddy boy, rockabilly, punk. At any one time, he has his consociates while others in the English scene not yet known are contemporaries. Shifts between the two categories occur frequently as one changes membership of subcultures and thus consociates or moves between quasi-groups within the skinhead subculture. The past consociates, now contemporaries, may again become consociates at some future point in time. The high frequency of meeting is due to the limited size of the English scene and its spatial location in known places. This transformative element is important if we are to use the concepts of consociates and contemporaries in the description of social relationships within labile groupings.

The synthesis of these concepts – action-set and quasi-group, scene and venue, specific memory and era, consociate and contemporary – provides an interlocking model of social processes in labile groupings. A skinhead joins an action-set. Its members visit a chosen scene, thus transforming it into a venue, and create a good night. This pattern of activity occurs for several weeks and the period becomes an era. Then the skinhead changes quasi-groups and begins associating with another group of skinheads. A different action-set is usually recruited and frequents a different venue to the original set. The skinhead has changed his quasi-group, his action-set and consociates, to find new consociates and to create new memories and perhaps eras. The skinheads of the original action-set have become contemporaries although the skinhead will probably meet up with them in various skinhead scenes.

Over several years, this process may occur several times. Not each change in quasi-group and action-set entails a change in social time and space. The new consociates may frequent the same venue and be a part of the same era as previous quasi-groups and action-sets. Changes in venue and era may also change without a corresponding change in consociates. The social residue of these described processes is a total, unbounded system which we may describe as the form of skinhead social life. Form is the product of process and can only be discerned through attention to this process. Form becomes a set of conditions for the maintenance, transformation and relegation of types of expressive social action. Such a conceptualization of the skinhead subculture and wider English scene allows for the study of social process. Within this process, there are certain types of expressive behaviour which are valued and judged. They give the social process between action-set and quasi-group cultural substance and prove that something worthwhile was achieved by skinhead terms of reference.

Authenticity and sincerity

Skinheads place great importance on consociate performance in skinhead activity. Authenticity is a judgement, collective or individual, made of this consociate activity and of personal and group performance in it. There is no explicit skinhead label for this quality, but perhaps 'hard' and 'hardness' come closest. Although being a skinhead involves three main activities: drinking, womanizing, and fighting, the concentration of labelling on fighting suggests the paramount importance of this third aspect. Fighting is essential, drinking and womanizing are not, although they are valued additions to the skinhead behavioural repertoire. While the archetypal skinhead participates in all three, fighting is the only indispensable element. Without it, skinhead identity cannot be claimed.

Trilling (1972, p. 93) asserts that authenticity applies to a person when the person's emotional state and expression of this emotional state are one and the same. For skinheads, authenticity is accorded when a particular skinhead is measured against an ideal subcultural type – the hard, loyal skinhead – and fares well in the comparison. He is considered to be an authentic skinhead because he fights well and wins; if he is also a womanizer and drinker so much the better.

Authenticity requires both the wearing of skinhead uniform and performance in the subculturally patterned modes of action signalled by this uniform. I presented a model for the judgement of authenticity in relation to the wearing of skinhead visual style in Chapter Three, that is, judgement within a moral world, a community of belonging. Smithy and Joe failed in their bid for authenticity because they failed to fulfil the second requirement of skinhead authenticity – performance in subculturally patterned modes of action with other skinheads. While Smithy, Joe, and the Oi! T-shirt wearer may appear skinheads to an undiscriminating public, and to a certain extent to the on-scene public (e.g., bouncers, hotel managers, other youth), they were denied this status by other skinheads, the real possessors of the knowledge about the criteria upon which such a judgement can be made. Skinheads police the ownership of their visual style.

There exists a second, no less important dimension to the judgement of skinheads by other skinheads – sincerity. Discussing an example will perhaps best demonstrate the difference between sincerity and authenticity. If a skinhead flees a dangerous situation leaving other skinheads to continue the battle alone, he will be challenged on one or both of two counts. The accusation may take the form of 'You call yourself a skinhead?' On this occasion of flight, the actor concerned has put his claim to skinhead authenticity at risk. Should the accusation be 'You call yourself a mate?' the deserting skinhead's sincerity is being questioned. The bestowal of sincerity is a more personal judgement which belongs to a closer relationship than the categorical 'skinhead', one between close consociates. The first judgement, that about authenticity, is made with reference to subculturally established expectations, that is, the judgement concerns one's ability to perform in subculturally patterned modes of action.

The second verdict, that about sincerity, is a judgement based on a particular relationship, usually between friends. Authenticity belongs to the understandings which unite the quasi-group. Sincerity belongs to the particular definition of relationships between persons who constitute an action-set. To be labelled insincere and unauthentic means that the accused has failed on both criteria and may result in ostracism.

In the example presented in Chapter Four, my actions in aiding Rhygin in the dangerous pub situation elicited the approval of Rhygin's skinhead mates. My claim was not to authenticity, for I was not a skinhead, but to sincerity. To use Trilling's (1972) definition, my avowal matched my actual feeling in the eyes of others. This congruence was tested in an actual situation and proved durable under threat. As Rhygin commented, when I told him of these conclusions, authenticity is less important than sincerity amongst close consociates. Rhygin has little need to prove his authenticity to Ace, Nutter, Jack or Roy for two reasons: these skinheads had been present on numerous occasions where he had demonstrated this authenticity, and his authenticity is, in part, established in a moral world which lies beyond them. His authenticity belongs to the category 'skinhead' where he is judged by skinheads at large in accordance with their categorical ideals about behaviour. When Ace, Nutter, Rhygin, Jack and Roy discussed past episodes of skinhead activity, they were demonstrating and reliving the sincerity of their commitment to each other. Their authenticity was not questioned. Authenticity belonged to stories of subcultural feats told to skinheads not as well-versed in the exploits of these particular persons. Judgement of one another, as members of an action-set, lay in the claiming and bestowal of sincerity.

In Chapters Four, Six and Seven I sketched the sorts of activities in which skinheads are expected to participate to claim authenticity. The most clear-cut of these is fighting side-by-side with fellow skinheads against others. These others can be divided into three groups: other skinheads, members of the English scene, and those drawn from outside the English scene. The ritual which informs these conflicts differs according to the identity of the protagonist(s). The greatest expression of authenticity is found in conflicts with outsiders because no network links are involved to complicate loyalty. Conflict between skinheads is avoided where possible as authenticity conflicts with sincerity. Skinhead versus skinhead means the supremacy of sincerity, deciding to support a close consociate against another skinhead, over authenticity, skinheads fighting side-by-side. The middle category of conflict, that between skinheads and members of the other subcultures which make up the English scene, involves a mixture of authenticity and sincerity depending on the identity of the protagonists. Should they be unknown, the opportunity to establish authenticity by fighting is presented. If an opponent is known then displays of sincerity may also figure in the conflict. There is some overlapping of territory. For example, a 'mate' should be loyal to friends in dangerous situations without necessarily being a skinhead.

Although there are two main forms for drinking, the heavy drinking session and the more sedate session (Chapter Six), only participation in the former may confer authenticity. The significance of the quiet session lies with evidence of one's sincerity. Heavy drinking is one element of the 'good night' ethos in which skinheads create the necessary means to fashion reputation. The chances of fighting (alongside other skinheads) and 'pulling a bird' increase greatly the more often one embarks on the Friday and Saturday night adventures which have as their focus heavy drinking. Heavy drinking is not, in any absolute sense, necessary for the fulfilment of these events except in confirming the ability to hold one's drink, nor do I wish to create the impression that excessive drinking is the motivating factor in activities which lead to the creation of 'memories'. The point is that drinking is a vital and recognized part of the night scene. Skinheads enter the potential good night aware of the possibilities – conflict with the police, casual sex, and clashes with members of hostile youth subcultures. Drinking provides a frame for these activities but it is not their cause.

A final means for the skinhead to establish his authenticity is to represent himself as an exploiter of women, primarily for sex, and to some extent to match these words with his actions (see Chapter Seven). But there is another aspect to these relationships. Skinheads may also develop strong emotional attachments to young women which complicate these categorical pronouncements. The difficult task, which few manage successfully, is to balance the public representations of the skinhead as exploiter and seeker of casual sex with the demands of a more complex relationship with a young woman.

As I have shown, the judgement of sincerity is relevant to violent situations but also to events less important at the subcultural level. I outlined several such events – Scouse's lack of pool-playing ability during the afternoon drinking session (Chapter Six), Pete's theft of the bottle of Clayton's, Terry's impersonation of the ocker Australian accent, and Rhygin's 'defeat' at the hands of the sixty-five-year-old man (all in Chapter Eight) – all of which have relevance only for the action-set. In the discussion of these events judgement is made of personal characteristics. A particular skinhead's personal identity becomes known to his action-set and quasi-group because of their witnessing of his actions or from their hearing about them through stories. Stories that elaborate on personal proclivities and characteristics hold little interest for those who do not know the actors personally.

Skinheads refuse to engage in debate about a person's inner motivational states. The reason for this absence of a domain of discussion in the skinhead world is that motivational discourse belongs to worlds of hierarchy and to formal structures in which role incumbents occupy positions of status. In this type of social structure, promotion and demotion may be effected with persons envisaged as motivational rather than as performative social types (Garfinkel 1956). By contrast, judgement in the labile skinhead subculture is brought down on its members through attention to performative success or failure in skinhead activity. Should someone fail to measure up to the requirements of authenticity, then he merely 'didn't have what it takes'. Little time is allocated in conversation to the reasons for this failure because it serves no purpose in the skinhead scheme to dwell on such matters. Instead, conversation tends to concentrate on the positive aspects of those who have succeeded in their pursuit of 'skinhead' status.

The outcome of sartorial commitment to skinhead uniform and to participation in skinhead activity is the creation of 'memories'. Memories are stories about skinhead good times, whether they be embellished accounts of violent events or about humorous situations. Having a fund of such stories to tell in group conversation achieves several things. Firstly, stories attest to skinhead authenticity on the part of those who are the subject of the stories. Tales of fights and of one's participation in drinking and the 'pulling of birds' (in good nights) are told to elicit the approval of other skinheads. The point is this: memories are about being and acting together with other skinheads. To possess a fund of such stories about one's participation with other skinheads in skinhead activity is to prove the authenticity of one's claim to be a skinhead. Yet one needs to be authentic to participate in the events that become the subject of memories. The process of becoming acknowledged collectively as a skinhead by other skinheads involves the interplay between authenticity and memories. The good time is the act, the story the evidence, and authenticity the verdict brought down on this act.

Secondly, stories of sincerity confirm friendships of the past and present. These stories about 'good laughs' are tales of idiosyncrasy, personality, and humour. These stories contribute little to subcultural or categorical reputation but celebrate friendship and validate skinhead leisure style as worthwhile. The history of performance as both a skinhead and a person is vested in memories. More generally, the telling of stories about desirable actions helps to produce a negotiated order (Strauss 1978) outlining what is and is not acceptable behaviour within the skinhead moral world.

Stories about events become the subject of memories to be relived and embellished in the future. They mark a skinhead's lengthy involvement in both the skinhead subculture and the English scene and also his authenticity and sincerity. The telling of stories usually occurs in a group context. Several skinheads may be sitting in a pub or at someone's house or flat, drinking. Inevitably, conversation turns to past good nights and good laughs. The history of consociation is vested in these memories.

Chapter Eight demonstrated that memories are of two main types: subcultural and personal. Subcultural memories relate to events concerning the performance of consociate skinhead activity. They represent skinhead action and in their telling and re-telling fame is manufactured, sustained and sometimes destroyed, if performance is deemed to be less than satisfactory. More often though, the telling of stories establishes authenticity and subcultural identity as a hard skinhead. Ace's reflection on Rhygin's head-butt as 'the best fuckin' head-butt I've ever seen!' marks Rhygin's fighting prowess. Likewise, the conversation about the good night described in Chapter Eight, concerning Billy, the skinhead who had a 'bit of aggro, pulled a bird, and got pissed', reinforced both Billy's ideal of authenticity and the subscription of those who participated in the night's events to this ideal. When a primary actor has been collectively judged as authentic, other skinheads, basking in vicarious glory, are also accorded this desired status. The explicit approval applies not only to Billy and his skinhead accomplices but also validates skinhead leisure style. The pattern of Billy's activities is reinforced because others were present to verify and judge it.

The second type of memory relates to more personal consociation. Good laughs add little to a skinhead's reputation as someone of subcultural note. Instead they mark the idiosyncrasies of person which exist apart from his skinhead identity. The incidents concerning

Scouse's poor pool-playing ability, Rhygin and the old man in the mall, Pete's theft of the bottle of Clayton's and Terry's humorous imitation of a moidy accent all signal individuality. While symbolic importance is attached to good nights, stories about good laughs mark possession of personal knowledge about other skinheads. They demonstrate friendship and concern the behaviour of those comprising the action-set.

Some memories relate to both performance in consociate skinhead and personal activity, that is, they have significance for one's subcultural identity (authenticity) and for one's personal identity among friends (sincerity). In Chapter Eight, I related some examples of this kind of memory. The practice of 'jumping taxis', the incident where several skinheads decided to pick fights with bogs 'for a laugh', and the long-running bet between several skinheads to 'get off with a bird you didn't know' all fall into this category. Because consociation involves both subcultural and personal actions the stories and judgement passed also reflect this intertwining of authenticity and sincerity. Analytically, the two strands can be separated but in social life many incidents and stories about incidents combine the two in differing proportions.

The dialectic operating within the social process of action-set and quasi-group, venue and scene, specific memory and era, and consociate and contemporary, also operates in the search for authenticity. Achieving authenticity necessitates movement around the skinhead and English scene to find good times. These good times then become one's evidence of authenticity. But there is a catch. Good times are no use if the good times constantly draw the attention of the police. Skinheads must fight to retain skinhead identity, but not so much as to become disillusioned with the scene and their categorical identity. The task is to balance skinhead opposition to the mainstream world, the search for 'trouble' and 'good times', with one's non-skinhead responsibilities – perhaps family relationships, a steady partner, or gaining employment. The balance becomes one of the allocation of one's time and energy to different sorts of relationships, broadly speaking, skinhead and non-skinhead. The successful skinhead balances both and is authentic and has a wide circle of consociates. When such responsibilities as a steady partner or a rapidly growing police record cause the skinhead to begin allocating more of his time to non-skinhead consociates and activities it is time for him to grow his hair.

There is one final dialectic operating at the broadest level. Being a skinhead involves a constant interplay between the subcultural level

– expressed in fighting, drinking and womanizing, and given explicit approval in judgements of authenticity – and the personal level – consisting of good laughs, quiet drinking and relationships with regular partners, and measured in terms of sincerity. For any single skinhead and for any set of skinheads the relationship between these two aspects of existence may differ greatly and may change from one set of events to the next.

Being a member of a youth subculture thus involves a dynamic process. Action-sets are transformed into quasi-groups and future action-sets are, in turn, drawn from the quasi-group. Specific memories are transformed into eras, and social relations with one set of consociates become transferred to another, thus rendering the past consociates contemporaries. The site of this social interaction moves from one venue, a specific scene, to the next. All these changes occur frequently over a period of several years, some of them at the same time. The expressive action occurring within this framework falls largely into two categories: consociate activity such as the good night, and more personal consociation such as the good laugh. Stories about these events become enshrined as memories which supply the evidence of one's authenticity and sincerity.

Implications

Rosaldo (1989), Sansom (1981), and Sass (1986) all discuss the growing crisis in anthropology which involves a rethinking of many of the discipline's tenets, particularly the problem of how to describe social process in the apparent absence of social structure and neatly defined social rules and rituals. The task of the anthropologist has become the description of social process, something the discipline is not well equipped to do. In the urban context, problems of conceptualization are highlighted by different, sometimes ephemeral and nebulous social arrangements. The problem for urban anthropology is how to shift from a focus on static social organization and structure to explain the dynamics of short-term arrangements, sets of people that defy the notion of arrangement in the accepted sense of the term. Building on Mayer's (1966) model of an Indian political election, Sansom's (1980) account of Darwin Aboriginal fringe-dwellers, and ethnographic material, I have provided a descriptive analysis of such a social grouping, an anthropology of social process.

Studies of English skinheads, and of other English youth subcultures, are marked by their attention to the historical and structural dimensions of social life. Analysis remains at the macro-sociological level and focuses on the meaning of youth subcultures within the English social class context. More recent critiques address problems of gender, ethnicity, and research method in the original formulations. While this cultural studies approach yields interesting findings, it necessitates a glossing-over of cultural analysis. While the behaviour of young people is partly a response to their structural position, it is surely negligent to end analysis at this point. English studies contribute little to our understanding of the phenomenology of skinhead, or other youth, subcultures – the nature of relationships between members of different subcultures, the social meaning of violence, questions of gender relations (although this deficit is being remedied), and the creation of identity through these activities. There is also little discussion of skinhead (or other youthful) social organization. One justification for the absence of such analysis is that it is trivial; that it is just window-dressing on the reality of social structure. In this view, issues relating to culture merely conceal underlying class relations. Anthony Cohen (1982, pp. 2-3), an anthropologist introducing a series of studies of British rural communities, disagrees:

> Some critics would certainly object that the postulation of diverse cultures in a closely integrated and predominantly urban-industrial political economy such as Britain is little more than mystification of superficial, and therefore trivial, differences. They would argue that such "aesthetic frills" (...) no more affect the working of state systems within the British Isles than the colour of its paintwork affects the running of a motor car. This is an argument couched in similar terms to those who object to the conceptualisation of "community" in such societies on the grounds either that local distinctiveness has been eliminated by ad-mass, or that "community" is merely symptomatic of the false consciousness which conceals the reality of class and state. Such arguments should not be treated as matters of ideological taste: they should be regarded as misunderstanding both society in Britain, and the very nature of culture.

How people perceive of their social situations must surely influence their actions and so it must be the legitimate task of any inquiry to unravel these understandings, from the point of view of those being studied. The social processes outlined in this book and the reasons for their perpetuation provide a point of departure for future investigations of youth.

145

English, Irish, Scottish and Welsh migrants are largely invisible in multicultural Australia. Although, when taken together, they comprise the largest migrant group in the country (1,127,196 persons at the 1986 Census), they are curiously neglected in debates over Australia's ethnic composition. Even to lump these four ethnic groups together is to gloss over the cultural, social, and historical differences between them and even within them (cf. Anthony Cohen 1982, p. 12). The skinheads of Perth comprise one particularly visible response to the English experience of migration to Australia but theirs is not an isolated response. Skinheads are one part of a youth scene characterized by several subcultures, the origins of which can be traced to England. At a wider level, skinheads are firmly enmeshed in an adult English community. Just as Italian, Greek and Vietnamese migrants construct hybrid and atavistic ethnic subcultures shaped by ideal visions of 'home', so too do English migrants although at a less visible level and only in particular social contexts. The task for future research is to outline some of the other ways in which this sometimes 'invisible' ethnicity is manifested in Australia and to put to rest the popular notion that only those from non-English speaking backgrounds are 'ethnic'.

Bibliography

Allen, R. (1970), *Skinhead*, New English Library, London.

_____ (1971), *Suedehead*, New English Library, London.

_____ (1972), *Skinhead Escapes*, New English Library, London.

Appleyard, R.T. (1964), *British Emigration to Australia*, Australian National University Press, Canberra.

Australian Bureau of Statistics (1986), *Census of Population and Housing*, Australian Government Publishing Service, Canberra.

Barbara, F., Usher, J. and Barnes, N. (1978), 'The rules of "shouting" in drinking groups in Sydney public bars', *Australian Journal of Social Issues*, 13, pp. 119-128.

Barnes, R. (1979), *Mods*, Eel Pie, London.

Barth, F. (1969), 'Introduction', in Barth, F. (ed.), *Ethnic Groups and Boundaries: The Social Organization of Culture Difference*, George Allen and Unwin, London, pp. 51-76.

Barthes, R. (1983), *The Fashion System*, Hill and Wang, New York.

Bell, D. (1990), *Acts of Union: Youth Culture and Sectarianism in Northern Ireland*, Macmillan, Basingstoke.

Bennet, L.A. and Ames, G.M. (eds) (1985), *The American Experience with Alcohol: Contrasting Cultural Perspectives*, Plenum, New York.

Bienen, H. (1968), *Violence and Social Change*, Chicago University Press, Chicago.

Blainey, G. (1984), *All for Australia*, Methuen Haynes, North Ryde.

Bloch, H. A. and Neiderhoffer, A. (1958), *The Gang: A Study in Adolescent Behaviour*, Philosophical Library, New York.

Bordieu, P. (1984), *Distinction*, Routledge and Kegan Paul, London.

Bordua, D. J. (1961), 'Delinquent subcultures: sociological interpretations of gang delinquency', *Annals*, 338, pp. 120-36.

Brake, M. (1974), 'The skinheads: an English working class culture', *Youth and Society*, 6, pp. 179-200.

_____ (1980), *The Sociology of Youth Culture and Youth Subcultures: Sex and Drugs and Rock 'n' Roll?*, Routledge and Kegan Paul, London.

_____ (1985), *Comparative Youth Culture*, Routledge and Kegan Paul, London.

Burke, K. (1945), *A Grammar of Motives*, Prentice-Hall, New York.

Burnley, I., Encel, S. and McCall, G. (eds) (1985), *Immigration and Ethnicity in the 1980s*, Longman Cheshire, Melbourne.

Burns, T.F. (1980), 'Getting rowdy with the boys', *Journal of Drug Issues*, 10, pp. 273-286.

Campbell, A. (1981), *Delinquent Girls*, Blackwell, Oxford.

_____ (1984), *The Girls in the Gang*, Blackwell, Oxford.

Cashmore, E. E. (1984), *No Future: Youth and Society*, Heinemann, London.

Castles, S., Cope, B., Kalantzis, M. and Morrissey, M. (1988), *Mistaken Identity: Multiculturalism and the Demise of Nationalism in Australia*, Pluto Press, Sydney.

Clarke, G. (1982), 'Defending ski-jumpers: a critique of theories of youth subcultures', *CCCS Stencilled Occasional Paper*, Sub and Popular Culture Series, SP No. 71.

Clarke, J. (1973a), 'The skinheads and the study of youth culture', *CCCS Stencilled Occasional Paper*, Sub and Popular Culture Series, SP No. 23.

_____ (1973b), 'Football hooliganism and the skinheads', *CCCS Stencilled Occasional Paper*, Sub and Popular Culture Series, SP No. 42.

_____ (1974), *Subcultural symbolism: reconceptualizing 'youth culture'*, unpublished M.A. Thesis, Centre for Contemporary Cultural Studies, University of Birmingham.

_____ and Jefferson, T. (1973a), 'The politics of popular culture: culture and sub-culture', *CCCS Stencilled Occasional Paper*, Sub and Popular Culture Series, SP No. 14.

_____ (1973b), 'Working class youth cultures'. *CCCS Stencilled Occasional Paper*, Sub and Popular Culture Series, SP No. 18.

Clifford, J. and Marcus, G.E. (eds) (1986), *Writing Culture: The Poetics and Politics of Ethnography*, University of California Press, Berkeley.

Cloward, R. A. and Ohlin, L. E. (1960), *Delinquency and Opportunity: A Theory of Delinquent Gangs*, Free Press, New York.

Cohen, Abner (ed.) (1974), *Urban Ethnicity*, Tavistock, London.

Cohen, Albert K. (1955), *Delinquent Boys: The Culture of the Gang*, Free Press, New York.

Cohen, Anthony (1982), 'Introduction', in Cohen, Anthony (ed.), *Belonging: Identity and Social Organization in British Rural Communities*, Institute of Social and Economic Research, Memorial University of Newfoundland, Social and Economic Papers No. 11.

Cohen, P. (1972), 'Sub-cultural conflict and working class community', *Working Papers in Cultural Studies*, 2 (Spring), pp. 5-51.

Cohen, R. (1978), 'Ethnicity: problem and focus in Anthropology', *Annual Review of Anthropology*, 7, pp. 379-403

Cohen, S. (1980), *Folk Devils and Moral Panics*, St Martin's Press, New York.

Colburn Jr., K. (1985), 'Honour, ritual and violence in ice hockey', *Canadian Journal of Sociology*, 10 (2), pp. 153-70.

Conway, R. (1971), *The Great Australian Stupor: An Interpretation of the Australian Way of Life*, Sun Books, Melbourne.

Daniel, S. and McGuire, P. (eds) (1972), *The Paint House: Words from an East End Gang*, Penguin, Harmondsworth.

Dennis, N., Henriques, F. and Slaughter, C. (1956), *Coal is our Life*, Eyre and Spottiswoode, London.

Dorn, N. (1983), *Alcohol, Youth and the State*, Croom Helm, London.

Downes, D. (1966), 'The gang myth', *Listener*, 75 (14 April), pp. 534-37.

Dunphy, D.C. (1969), *Cliques, Crowds and Gangs: Group Life of Sydney Adolescents*, Cheshire, Melbourne.

Dyck, N. (1980), 'Booze, barrooms and scrapping: masculinity and violence in a Western Canadian town', *Canadian Journal of Anthropology*, 1 (2), pp. 191-98.

Ferguson, J. (1982), 'Jim Ferguson's fashion notebook', in Knight, N. (ed.), *Skinhead*, Omnibus, London, pp. 36-47.

Fine, G. A. and Kleinman, S. (1979), 'Rethinking subculture: an interactionist analysis', *American Journal of Sociology*, 85 (1), pp. 1-20.

Finestone, H. (1957), 'Cats, kicks and colour', in Baxter, P. and Sansom, B. (eds) (1972), *Race and Social Difference*, Penguin, Harmondsworth, pp. 423-40.

Fiske, J., Hodge, B. and Turner, G. (1987), *Myths of Oz: Reading Australian Popular Culture*, Allen and Unwin, Sydney.

Foley, D. (1988), 'Does the working class have a culture in the anthropological sense?', *Cultural Anthropology*, 4(2), pp. 137-162.

Fox, R. (1976), 'The inherent rules of violence', in Collet, P. (ed.), *Social Rules and Social Behaviour*, Blackwell, Oxford, pp. 132-49.

Frith, S. (1981), 'Hooked on love', *New Society*, 23, pp. 152-153.

_____ (1984), *The Sociology of Youth*, Causeway, Ormskirk.

Fyvel, T. R. (1961), *The Insecure Offenders: Rebellious Youth in the Welfare State*, Chatto and Windus, London.

Garfinkel, H. (1956), 'Conditions of successful status degradation ceremonies', *American Journal of Sociology*, 61 (5), pp. 420-24.

Geertz, C. (1966), *Person, Time and Conduct in Bali*, Cultural Report Series No. 14, Southeast Asia Studies, Yale University.

_____ (1972), 'Deep play: notes on a Balinese cockfight', *Daedalus*, 101, pp. 1-37.

Granovetter, M. S. (1973), 'The strength of weak ties', *American Journal of Sociology*, 78, pp. 1360-80.

_____ (1983), 'The strength of weak ties: a network theory revisited', in Collins, R. (ed.), *Sociological Theory*, Jossey-Bass, San Francisco, pp. 201-33.

Hall, S. and Jefferson, T. (1976), *Resistance Through Rituals*, Hutchinson, Birmingham.

Hannerz, U. (1969), *Soulside: Inquiries into Ghetto Culture and Community*, Columbia University Press, New York.

_____ (1980), *Exploring the City: Inquiries Toward an Urban Anthropology*, Columbia University Press, New York.

Hebdige, D. (1974a), 'The style of the Mods', *CCCS Stencilled Occasional Paper*, Sub and Popular Culture Series, SP No. 20.

_____ (1974b), 'Reggae, rastas and rudies: style and the subversion of form', *CCCS Stencilled Occasional Paper*, Race Series, SP No. 24.

_____ (1979), *Subculture: The Meaning of Style*, Methuen, London.

_____ (1982), 'This is England! And they don't live here', in Knight, N. (ed.), *Skinhead*, Omnibus, London, pp. 26-35.

Hepburn, J.R. (1973), 'Violent behaviour in interpersonal relationships', *The Sociological Quarterly*, 14 (Summer), pp. 419-29.

Hewitt, R. (1986), *White Talk Black Talk: Inter-racial Friendship and Communication Amongst Adolescents*, Cambridge University Press, Cambridge.

Hill, T.W. (1974), 'From hell-raiser to family man', in Spradley, J.P. and McCurdy, D.W. (eds), *Conformity and Conflict: Readings in Cultural Anthropology*, 2nd Edition, Little, Brown and Co., Boston, pp. 186-200.

Horne, D. (1964), *The Lucky Country*, Penguin, Ringwood.

Horowitz, R. and Schwartz, G. (1974), 'Honor, normative ambiguity and gang violence', *American Sociological Review*, 39, pp. 238-51.

Houghton, D.S. (1979), *Perth at the 1976 Census: A Social Atlas*, Department of Geography, University of Western Australia, Perth.

Hunt, G. and Satterlee, S. (1983), 'Cohesion and division: drinking in an English village', *Man*, 21, pp. 521-37.

Ireland, D. (1982), *The Glass Canoe*, Penguin, Ringwood.

Jefferson, T. (1973), 'The Teds – a political resurrection', *CCCS Stencilled Occasional Paper*, Sub and Popular Culture Series, SP No. 22.

Journal of Research into Crime and Delinquency, 4(1), (1967). Special edition on delinquency.

Kapferer, B. (1988), *Legends of People, Myths of State*, Smithsonian Institute Press, Washington.

Keiser, R. L. (1969), *The Vice Lords: Warriors of the Streets*, Holt, Rinehart and Winston, New York.

Knight, N. (ed.) (1982), *Skinhead*, Omnibus, London.

Laing, D. (1985), *One Chord Wonders – Power and Meaning in Punk Rock*, Open University Press, Milton Keynes.

Liebow, E. (1967), *Tally's Corner: A Study of Streetcorner Men*, Little, Brown and Co., Boston.

Lorenz, K. (1970), *On Aggression*, Methuen, London.

MacAndrew, C. and Edgerton, R.B. (1969), *Drunken Comportment: A Social Explanation*, Aldine, Chicago.

MacDonald, Hales and Associates (1989), *Diversity is Great, Mate!: A Study of Community Relations in an Inner-City Area of Perth, Western Australia*, Multicultural and Ethnic Affairs Commission, Perth.

McGregor, A. (1967), *Profile of Australia*, Penguin, Harmondsworth.

McGuigan, J. (1992), *Cultural Populism*, Routledge, London.

McRobbie, A. (1978), 'Working class girls and the culture of femininity', in Women's Study Group (ed.), *Women Take Issue*, Hutchinson, London, pp. 96-108.

_____ (1980), 'Settling accounts with subcultures: a feminist critique', *Screen Education*, 34, pp. 37-50.

_____ (1991), *Feminism and Youth Culture: From Jackie to Just Seventeen*, Macmillan, Basingstoke.

_____ and Garber, J. (1976), 'Girls and subcultures', in Hall, S. and Jefferson, T. (eds), *Resistance Through Rituals*, Hutchinson, London, pp. 209-22.

Marcus, G.E. (1986), 'Contemporary problems of ethnography in the modern world system', in Clifford, J. and Marcus, G.E. (eds), *Writing Culture: The Poetics and Politics of Ethnography*, University of California Press, Berkeley, pp. 165-193.

Markus, A. and Ricklefs, M.C. (eds) (1985), *Surrender Australia?: Essays in the Study and Uses of History; Geoffrey Blainey and Asian Immigration*, George Allen and Unwin, Sydney.

Marsh, P. (1978), *Aggro*, Dent, London.

_____, Rosser, E. and Hame, R. (1978), *The Rules of Disorder*, Routledge and Kegan Paul, London.

Marshall, G. (1991), *Spirit of '69: A Skinhead Bible*, S.T. Publishing, Dunoon.

Marsland, D. (1978), *Sociological Explorations in the Service of Youth*, National Youth Board, Leicester.

Marx, E. (1976), *The Social Context of Violent Behaviour*, Routledge and Kegan Paul, London.

Mayer, A. (1966), 'The significance of quasi-groups in the study of complex societies', in Banton, M. (ed.), *The Social Anthropology of Complex Societies*, Tavistock Publications, London, pp. 97-122.

Metcalfe, A. (1985), 'The day the workers went on strike because the sun did shine', *Social Analysis*, 17 (August), pp. 3-16.

Middleton, P. (1986), 'For "Victorian" read "Georgian": Mrs Thatcher corrected', *Encounter*, 67 (2), pp. 5-9.

Miller, W.B. (1958), 'Lower class culture as a generating milieu of gang delinquency', *Journal of Social Issues*, 14, pp. 5-19.

Mitchell, J. C. (1956), *The Kalela Dance*, Manchester University Press, Manchester.

Moore, D. (1990), 'Drinking, the construction of ethnic identity and social process in a Western Australian youth subculture', *British Journal of Addiction*, 85, pp. 1265-1278.

Moore, P. (1991), *Subcontracting in Perth: An Urban Ethnography*, unpublished doctoral dissertation, Department of Anthropology, University of Western Australia.

Multicultural and Ethnic Affairs Commission of Western Australia (1989), *Annual Report (1988-1989)*, MEACWA, Perth.

Mungham, G. and Pearson, G. (eds) (1976), *Working Class Youth Culture*, Routledge and Kegan Paul, London.

Oetting, E.R. and Beauvais, F. (1988), 'Common elements in youth drug abuse: peer clusters and other psychosocial factors', in Peele, S. (ed.), *Visions of Addiction: Major Contemporary Perspectives on Addiction and Alcoholism*, D.C. Heath and Co., Lexington, pp. 141-161.

Oxley, H. (1978), *Mateship in Local Organisation*, University of Queensland Press, St Lucia.

Parker, H. (1974), *View from the Boys*, David and Charles, Newton Abbot.

Patrick, J. (1973), *A Glasgow Gang Observed*, Methuen, Eyre.

Pearson, K. (1979), *Surfing Subcultures of Australia and New Zealand*, University of Queensland Press, St Lucia.

Polsky, N. (1971), *Hustlers, Beats and Others*, Aldine, Chicago.

Redhead, S. (1990), *The End of the Century Party: Youth and Pop Towards 2000*, Manchester University Press, Manchester.

Richardson, A. (1974), *British Immigrants and Australia: A Psychological Inquiry*, Australian National University Press, Canberra.

Roberts, B. (1973), 'Parent and youth cultures: alternative views: A critique of the work of Cohen, Cloward and Ohlin, Sykes and Matza', *CCCS Stencilled Occasional Paper*, Sub and Popular Culture Series, SP No. 28.

Room, R. (1985), 'Foreword', in Bennet, L.A. and Ames, G.M. (eds), *The American Experience with Alcohol: Contrasting Cultural Perspectives*, Plenum, New York, pp. xi-xvii.

Rosaldo, R. (1989), *Culture and Truth: The Remaking of Social Analysis*, Beacon Press, Boston.

Sansom, B. (1980), *The Camp at Wallaby Cross*, Australian Institute of Aboriginal Studies, Canberra.

_____ (1981), 'Processural modellings and aggregate groupings in Northern Australia', in Holy, M. and Stutchlik, L. (eds), *The Anthropology of Folk Models*, Academic Press, London, pp. 257-80.

Sargent, M. (1973), *Alcoholism as a Social Problem*, University of Queensland Press, St Lucia.

Sass, L. (1986), 'Anthropology's native problems', *Harpers*, 272 (May), pp. 49-57.

Sato, I. (1991), *Kamikaze Biker: Parody and Affluence in Affluent Japan*, University of Chicago Press, Chicago.

Schutz, A. (1962), *The Problem of Social Reality. Collected Papers, Vol. 1*, M.M. Nijhoff, The Hague.

Scott, P. (1956), 'Gangs and delinquent groups in London', *British Journal of Delinquency*, 7 (July), pp. 8-21.

Shergold, P. and Milne, F. (1984), *The Great Immigration Debate*, Ethnic Communities Council, New South Wales.

Short, J. F. (1968), *Gang Delinquency and Delinquent Subcultures*, Harper and Row, New York.

Stratton, J. (1992), *The Young Ones: Working-Class Culture, Consumption and the Category of Youth*, Black Swan Press, Perth.

Strauss, A. (1978), *Negotiations*, Jossey-Bass Publishers, London.

Taylor, I. (1971), 'Soccer consciousness and soccer hooliganism', in Cohen, S. (ed.), *Images of Deviance*, Penguin, Harmondsworth, pp. 134-64.

Thrasher, F. M. (1927), *The Gang: A Study of 1,313 Gangs in Chicago*, University of Chicago Press, Chicago.

Tiger, L. (1972), *Men in Groups*, Panther, London.

Toch, H. (1969), *Violent Men*, Aldine, Chicago.

Trilling, L. (1972), *Sincerity and Authenticity*, Oxford University Press, London.

Walker, J.C. (1985), 'Rebels with our applause? A critique of resistance theory in Paul Willis's ethnography of schooling', *Journal of Education*, 167(2), pp. 63-83.

_____ (1986), 'Romanticizing resistance, romanticizing culture: problems in Willis's theory of cultural production', *British Journal of Sociology of Education*, 7(1), pp. 59-80.

_____ (1988), *Louts and Legends: Male Youth Culture in an Inner City School*, Allen and Unwin, Sydney.

Wallman, S. (1986), 'Ethnic and boundary process in context', in Rex, J. and Mason, D. (eds), *Theories of Race and Ethnic Relations*, Cambridge University Press, Cambridge, pp. 226-245 .

Walter, E.V. (1969), *Terror and Resistance: A Study of Political Violence*, Oxford University Press, New York.

Ward, R. (1966), *The Australian Legend*, Oxford University Press, Melbourne.

Waters, C. (1981), 'Badges of half-formed inarticulate radicalism: a critique of recent trends in the study of working-class culture', *International Labour and Working Class History*, 19 (Spring), pp. 23-37.

White, R. (1990), *No Space of Their Own: Young People and Social Control in Australia*, Cambridge University Press, Sydney.

Willis, P. (1977), *Learning to Labour*, Saxon House, London.

_____ (1978), *Profane Culture*, Routledge and Kegan Paul, London.

_____ (1990), *Common Culture: Symbolic Work at Play in the Everyday Cultures of the Young*, Open University Press, Milton Keynes.

Wilson, D. (1978), 'Sexual codes and conduct: a study of teenage girls', in Smart, C. and Smart, B. (eds), *Women, Sexuality and Social Control*, Routledge and Kegan Paul, London, pp. 65-73.

Wilson, P. (1980), *Drinking in England and Wales*, HMSO, London.

Wrennall, L. (1986), 'The "Turbo Kids"', *Youth Studies Bulletin*, 5(2), pp. 4-8.

Yablonsky, L. (1959), 'The delinquent gang as a near-group', *Social Problems*, 7 (Fall), pp. 108-17.

_____ (1963), *The Violent Gang*, Macmillan, New York.

Zamoyska, B. (1987), *The Ten Pound Fare: Experiences of British People Who Migrated to Australia in the 1950s*, Viking, London.

Index

Clifford, J. 118n.6
Cloward, R.A. 33n.2
Cohen, Abner 11
Cohen, Albert K. 33n.2
Cohen, Anthony 19, 33, 145, 146
Cohen, P. 1, 7, 9
Cohen, R. 10
Cohen, S. 8, 21n.7, 84
Colburn Jr. K. 79, 81n.1
consociate(s) 86-88
   activity 17, 20
   experience 63, 112
      young women and 113
   identity 79, 119-120, 132
   intermittent 24
   occasional 24
   regular 24
contemporaries 86-88
Conway, R. 101n.2
Cope, B. 5n.1
crocodile hunters, Australian
   82n.7
cultural construction 2

Daniel, S. 8
day skinheads 19, 43, 49-50
   drinking and 94-95
definition of the situation 10
Dennis, N. 101
domains, recreation 20
   leisure 61
Dorn, N. 101
Downes, D. 23-24
drinking 29
   dramaturgical perspective on
   91
   ethnicity and 97-99
   (non)round 99-101
   styles of 91-95
Dunphy, D. 33n.2
Dyck, N. 81n.1

Edgerton, R. 97
egalitarianism 11, 97, 100
Encel, S. 5n.1

English skinheads 1, 2, 7, 21n.2,
   84
   analyses of 7-8
   and amphetamine use 7
   and assaults on gays 7
      hippies 7
      Pakistani immigrants 7
   drinking 7
   mark one 8
   mark two 8
   studies of 145
   visual style 36-43
   working-class base of 46
English migrants, assimilation of
   children of 13
   adult 12
era(s) 25, 29-30, 68, 84, 85, 87, 121
ethnicity, and visual style 46-48
   drinking and 97-99
   English in Australia 20
   in Australia 2-3
   invisible 3, 146
   white 8
ethnographic authority 118n.6
ethnography 3-5, 9
ex-mods 83
'ex-skin(heads)' 14, 25, 27, 32, 46-
   47, 66, 71, 73, 83, 85

fashion, notion of 43
feminist critique of youth studies
   8, 117n.1
Ferguson, J. 36, 63n.1
fighting 28, 29, 92, 113, 123-125
   'fair' 79-80
   young women and 113-114
Fine, G.A. 17-19
Finestone, H. 60, 64n.8
Fiske, J. 101n.2
fleeting associations 24
Foley, D. 21n.7

football 87
  Australian Rules 14
  English supporters 64n.4
  hooliganism 7
  in Australia 22n.9
  Perth clubs 11, 13
  violence 21n.3
  visiting British teams 47
formulating place 59
Fox, R. 81n.1
Frith, S. 8, 117n.5
Fyvel, T.R. 20n.1

gangs 23-25, 33n.1
Garber, J. 8, 117n.1
Garfinkel, H. 141
Geertz, C. 6n.3, 86, 89n.1
'good laugh(s)' 120, 126-130
'good night(s)' 20, 28, 29, 68, 119-126
Granovetter, M. 18, 24
grey market in clothing 45

Hall, S. 21n.5
Hame, R. 64n.4, 81n.1
Hannerz, U. 20, 32, 34n.6, 61, 84, 115, 117n.1
'hard(ness)' 63, 65-66, 78-79, 81n.2, 131
Hebdige, D. 7, 8, 15, 20n.1, 21n.2, 21n.5, 35, 36, 46, 63, 84
Henriques, F. 101
Hepburn, J.R. 81n.1
Hewitt, R. 21n.4
Hill, T.W. 89n.2
hippies 84
Hodge, B. 101n.2
Horne, D. 101n.2
Horowitz, R. 82n.6
Houghton, D. 10
Hunt, G. 99, 101

ice hockey players 79-80
identity 119
  consociate 79, 119-120, 132

construction/creation of 20, 130-133
ethnic 11, 12
  drinking and 91-101
performative 79
personal 11, 33, 48, 86, 120, 127, 130-133
  sexuality and 116
  young women and 112-113
self-liquidating 24, 54, 100
subcultural/categorical
skinhead 28, 48, 51, 53, 54, 55, 56, 57, 66, 77, 80, 81, 100, 110, 120, 130-133
intoxication 93-94, 97
Ireland, D. 101n.2
Italianite style 7

Jefferson, T. 20n.1, 21n.5
Journal of Research into Crime and Delinquency 33n.1
'jumping taxis' 129

Kalantzis, M. 5n.1
Kapferer, B. 97
Keiser, L. 23
Kleinman, S. 17-19
Knight, N. 7, 43, 117n.3, 133n.1
known identities 46-47, 131

lability 15-17, 52
Laing, D. 21n.7
larrikinism 33n.2
Liebow, E. 25, 110
Lorenz, K. 81n.1

MacAndrew, C. 97
McCall, G. 5n.1
MacDonald, Hales and Associates 5n.1, 10, 11
McGregor, A. 101n.2
McGuigan, J. 9
McGuire, P. 8
McRobbie, A. 8, 21n.7, 115, 117n.1